REAL MONEY

FOR

Free People

THE AMERICAN GOLD STORY

JIM CLARK

*This book is dedicated to the memory of the late
John L. Niehaus, a friend and a mentor.*

CONTENTS

Preface

1: The Money Madmen   **1**

2: Real Money - Free People   **11**

3: The Free Republic is Born   **21**

4: Why Gold?   **29**

5: Why Silver?   **37**

6: The Federal Reserve   **45**

7: Stealing the People's Gold   **57**

8: Goodbye to Gold   **69**

9: So Long, Silver!   **79**

10: The End Game   **87**

Appendix I: Gold vs. Silver   **97**

Appendix II: Republic Monetary Exchange   **103**

Appendix III: About the Author   **107**

PREFACE

Someone wise once said that while life must be lived in forward, it only makes sense in reverse. I do not know if looking back is always the only way to make sense of things, but there is something to be said for marveling at the circumstances and events that have gotten us where we are in life.

I have spent most of my life in the precious metals business. I have been in the day-to-day thick of the markets when wars broke out and revolutions toppled world leaders. From my position on the trading desk, I have watched the markets rattle as major companies and entire countries have gone bankrupt. I played a part in one of the most audacious events in the modern history of precious metals.

Through the years I have had the pleasure of working with some truly extraordinary and even brilliant people. My company and my employees have served many thousands of clients, helping them protect their wealth and profit from the folly of our times. Many of those clients, more than I can count, have become friends, some casual, some close, all appreciated. I have been able to comfortably support my family with work that I genuinely love. And I have learned more than I ever could have expected to learn along the way.

It is for those reasons, and many other blessings that I have not mentioned, that at this point in my life I have been remembering with deep gratitude the improbable connections that led me almost a half century ago to a lifetime in the gold and silver business.

Quite by chance I had a high school girlfriend in 1972 whose father had a gold and silver dealership. He was a gifted and farsighted man, pioneering in the precious metals brokerage industry that was in its infancy: President Nixon had just uncoupled the dollar from gold a year earlier. Because Americans were forbidden by federal law from owning monetary gold, the industry was growing up around numismatic (collector) and foreign coins that could bypass this perfectly absurd restriction on the rights of the people. And because President Johnson had removed silver from America's coinage a few years earlier, farsighted investors began to take note of silver's prospects as well.

My girlfriend's father noted my interest in his work, and when I was fresh out of high school in 1973, at the age of eighteen, he offered me a job as a vault clerk in his Phoenix gold and silver brokerage. The high school romance ended the way these things often do, but the career that it launched me on continued. Although I left his company after a little more than a year to be principal of a new company, I remain so grateful after all this time to John Niehaus, since deceased, for the start he gave me and all he taught me, that I am dedicating this book to his memory.

It is my hope that with this book I can in some way "pay it forward." That just as the changing acquaintances and circumstance of life that brought me to this point—much closer to the end of my story than the beginning—this small book will play a significant role in your own life; that the lessons I have learned and share here will give you a new understanding of the mysteries of money and protect you from the fate of those who through the centuries have discovered too late that governments cannot be trusted with responsibility for the monetary systems of free people; that it will manipulate money matters to the advantage of the State at the expense of the people; and that there are reasons why gold and silver are the enduring money of the ages and should be inseparable from the American monetary system.

CHAPTER ONE
THE MONEY MADMEN

Gideon Gono does not look like a man you would single out at a glance as an idiot or a crazy person. He looks intelligent enough. There is no hysterical giggle with eyes darting wildly about that would cause him to be remembered through the ages as a madman.

But looks can be deceiving.

For a long time to come, when people speak about monetary madness Gideon Gono's name will come up. He is the man who made his nation an international laughingstock. Monetary historians and hobbyists keep evidence of his handiwork framed on their office walls.

This author has evidence of Gideon Gono's achievements tucked away in a drawer somewhere: a 100,000,000,000,000 Zimbabwean dollar bill. That is, a one-hundred-trillion-dollar bank note issued by the central bank of Zimbabwe in 2008. It is the highest denomination that has ever graced a nation's paper money.

The hyperinflationary Zimbabwe dollar has all the characteristics of a modern currency. It is printed on a fine paper stock, with carefully engraved scroll work. It has both a serial number and a security strip running through it. There are also authenticating marks that are disclosed under ultraviolet black light. It bears iconic Zimbabwean images: the balancing rocks at Epworth on the obverse, and cascading Victoria Falls and a cape buffalo on the reverse.

It is all very dignified and official. It also bears the signature of the governor of the Reserve Bank of Zimbabwe, Dr. G. Gono.

The numbers that describe Zimbabwe's monetary practices are so astronomical that the exact details hardly matter, but by 2009 the Zimbabwe dollar/US dollar exchange was Z$2,621,984,228,675,650,147, 435,579,309,984,228 to US$1. That would be said as 2 decillion, 621 nonillion, 984 octillion, 228 septillion, 675 sextillion, 650 quintillion, 147 quadrillion, 435 trillion, 579 billion, 309 million, 984 thousand, 228 Zimbabwe dollars in exchange for one US dollar. Gideon Gono was printing money as fast as he could to stave off national bankruptcy.

But Zimbabwe was already bankrupt. Its people were trillionaires who could not afford their next meal. Carrying trillion-dollar notes, they began asking one another what comes after "quadrillion." The currency was not worth the paper it was printed on. Indeed, the printing made perfectly good paper worthless.

Price controls are an inevitable accompaniment to inflation. But with the prices of the staples of life fixed below their cost of production, the store shelves in Zimbabwe soon emptied. Black markets developed with goods priced in foreign currencies. Without them and the primitive and inefficient barter that sprang up, commerce might have stopped completely. As for Gono, he made it his personal business to discover shopkeepers who violated his price-fixing edicts and have them arrested.

And at the end of a long day of arrests and currency destruction, Gideon Gono would retire to his forty-seven-bedroom mansion in Harare.

Gono does not appear to be a raving lunatic. In official testimony he speaks like any self-respecting bureaucrat about things like "administrative functions," setting up "various committees," and pleading for resources.

In printing money like this, said Gono, who spent ten years as head of the central bank, he was not doing anything the major central banks of the world were not doing.

He had a point.

Gono claims that he was offered the vice presidency of the World Bank in 2005, with the blessings of President George W. Bush, Secretary of State Condoleezza Rice, and the World Bank itself. We do not know how to judge the veracity of that claim. If so, it would have been characteristically bad judgement by Bush, who actually did install Iraq war architect Paul Wolfowitz as the head of the World Bank in 2005. Among Wolfowitz's serial absurdities was the claim that the Iraq war would pay for itself.

"There is a lot of money to pay for this that doesn't have to be US taxpayer money, and it starts with the assets of the Iraqi people," said then Deputy Secretary of Defense Wolfowitz in 2003 House testimony. "We're dealing with a country that could really finance its own reconstruction, and relatively soon."

Not a word of it was true. But who cares? The US, under both Republicans and Democrats, just printed the money for its elective Iraq war and its other serial regime-change wars.

But the US did not learn about money printing from Gideon Gono. So thoroughly Gonoist were the monetary authorities of the US even before Gono introduced his first new Zimbabwe dollar, that the Federal Reserve flew $12 billion in cash of uncertain provenance to Iraq in 2003–2004. Shrink-wrapped, washing machine-sized pallets of freshly printed $100 bills.

It went to Paul Bremer, the American in charge of the occupation of Iraq. And it disappeared. At least $9 billion. Without records. Without accounting. It went into gym bags and hidey holes. It went into the trunks of cars and into the private safes of Iraqi officials. It went to ghost employees and to American contractors that had no experience doing the things they were purportedly paid to do. It went into gunny sacks and down ratholes.

It just went.

Who cares? They can always print more.

Said Paul Bremer, "Our top priority was to get the economy moving again. The first step was to get money into the hands of the Iraqi people as quickly as possible."

Pure Gonoism.

VENEZUELA

Q: *How many Venezuelan bolivars does it take to buy an ounce of gold?*

A: *Who cares?*

It is a good joke because no one we know, or can reasonably imagine, would be willing to trade perfectly good gold for bolivars, knowing full well that the bolivars taken in exchange today will likely be worth much, much less tomorrow.

But the condition of the Venezuelan economy and the suffering of the Venezuelan people is hardly the stuff of jokes. It is a human horror story only made worse by the fact that it is not the result of some unavoidable natural disaster like a flood or an earthquake. The deprivation forced on the country's 28 million people is manmade. It was entirely foreseeable. And entirely unnecessary.

It is the inevitable consequence of policy choices made by Venezuela's autocrats Hugo Chávez and Nicolás Maduro and their henchmen of the left.

Judging by conditions today, it is hard to believe the Venezuela was the fourth richest economy in the world in the 1950s. But there is no prosperity so great—even with the world's largest oil reserves—that socialism and its monetary management cannot destroy. That explains why more than five million people have fled the country in its prevailing destitution. Venezuela's economic collapse remains a work in progress, and its humanitarian suffering persists.

Venezuela's annual inflation rate reached 816 percent in 2015, 1,906 percent in 2017 and 3,275 percent in May 2020, according to the studies of Steven Hanke of Johns Hopkins University.

The growth of the monetary base is one means of measuring a central bank's money printing. In the fall of 2019, Venezuela's monetary base had grown 73,000 percent over the prior 12 months.

In tracking Venezuela's inflation in 2017, the year that the country introduced its 100,000-bolivar bill, Professor Hanke and a colleague wrote, "Venezuela, welcome to the record books. You have now entered the inglorious sphere of hyperinflation. It is a world of economic chaos, wrenching poverty, and death. Its purveyors should be incarcerated, and the keys should be thrown away."

It is too late to lock up Hugo Chávez for his leading role in the destruction of Venezuela's economy; the former president died in 2012; but his successor Nicolás Maduro is still available for imprisonment.

And Gideon Gono is still walking around free in Zimbabwe.

THE WEIMAR REPUBLIC

A Zimbabwe here and a Venezuela there. But I would not want to create the impression that only third world countries fall prey to monetary madness. It is not the spawn of illiterate people in backwater lands. The derangement can easily strike modern and powerful industrial economies, and nations of educated people.

I keep my Zimbabwe dollars in an envelope with currency samples from a modern, industrial European nation. The German inflation of the 1920s was another one for the books. A 50,000-mark Reichsbank note bears the same characteristics of Zimbabwe's currency more than eighty yeas later: a fine bank note stock, with highly detailed scrollwork engraving, colored ink, serial numbers, signatures, and seals. It is a formidable looking currency, about 4 5/8 inches high, 7 ½ inches wide. It is dated November 1922.

I have another, much the same, dated a few months later, in February 1923, but it is for 100,000 marks. Not long after, as the inflation roared along, the denominations rose to the millions. I have one-, two-, and ten-million-mark notes. Thanks to the highly vaunted German efficiency of the era, that national bank began printing the new notes on cheaper, flimsy stock, notes less than half the size of the earlier currency. And to really economize on the money printing, it began printing the notes on only one side of the paper.

If the comic-tragedy of Zimbabwe's inflation was the work of one man, it was one running a national central bank. Gideon Gono (or perhaps Gono as the doppelganger of Zimbabwe's Marxist tyrant president Robert Mugabe), manned the levers of monetary policy mostly by himself. But the frenzied money printing that paved the way for the national socialist nightmare to come in the Germany of the 1920s was the work of a succession of statist bureaucrats at the national central bank.

Chief among them was Rudolf von Havenstein. Von Havenstein was a lawyer and a judge before becoming the head of the Reichsbank where he oversaw the hyperinflationary nightmare of 1919 to 1923.

At the beginning of the period one gold mark was worth about 100 paper German marks. By November 1923, one gold mark was equal to about 100 trillion paper German marks. It cost 36 billion marks to send a postcard from Munich to Prague. The cost of a loaf of bread, only about one mark before the debacle, eventually rose to 200 billion marks. No wonder: at the peak of the madness there were 30 paper mills, 150 printing firms, and 2,00o noisy printing presses cranking out von Havenstein's currency.

It makes today's quiet and easy electronic money printing look positively sophisticated, although ours is the same old flim-flam dressed up for the digital age. Unbacked currency, whether paper or digital, is not wealth. It is instead only an accounting fraud, one that masks its intended function of transferring wealth.

Despite the license to print currency without limitation, the German State was so desperate for currency other than its own, that in September 1923 police raided restaurants and nightclubs in Berlin, searching the wallets and purses of customers for foreign cash.

As conditions deteriorated, one Berlin newspaper asked if von Havenstein understood that Germany's workers could starve. But Havenstein insisted all along that prices spinning out of control and the mark's collapsing exchange rate were unrelated to his furious money-printing. At the end of the monetary tragedy von Havenstein died, apparently coincidentally.

The affair decimated the German economy and radicalized the people. Crime proliferated: gasoline was siphoned from parked cars; prostitution flourished; urban dwellers stormed the farms of the countryside looking for food. With the social fabric shredded, the central bank's benchmark interest rate at 90 percent, and the unemployment rate nearing 25 percent (soon to be 30 percent), the first of the Nazis' infamous Nuremberg rallies was held in September 1923. Thirty-four-year-old Adolf Hitler spoke to a crowd a hundred thousand strong.

Did von Havenstein really not know what he was doing as he crushed the German economy? Or did he just inflate the currency to worthlessness at the time because he felt he had no other choice? Was he afraid higher interest rates would do to the economy what he himself did? Was he afraid of a Bolshevik revolution? Or did he just find himself holding the hammer of the currency printing press and, looking around, decide that every problem looked like a nail?

In any case, it reminds one of the head of our own central bank, Federal Reserve chairman Jerome Powell. About printing money electronically at unprecedented rates in 2020, Powell said, "We're not even thinking about thinking about the consequences of our actions."

Neither was von Havenstein.

Neither was Gideon Gono.

Fed chairman Powell said that the Fed has "crossed a lot of red lines that had not been crossed before." But, he said, "you do that and you figure it out afterward."

Figure it out afterward? That sounds to us like Scarlett O'Hara oversees monetary policy. "Fiddle-de-dee! I'll think about that tomorrow!"

Nothing the Fed has done has fixed anything. Like Gideon Gono and von Havenstein, the money printers only push the confrontation with financial reality a little farther down the road. By then, the US dollar and debt problems will be bigger. The collapse will be even more destructive.

Could Gideon Gono be forgiven his folly because of ignorance? He was only *Doctor* Gono because of a sketchy degree conferred on him by a sketchy institution. But Powell had what passes as the finest education the West has to offer. He went to Georgetown Prep. He has a degree from Princeton. Like von Havenstein, Powell is a lawyer. His juris doctorate degree is from Georgetown, where he edited the law journal. Neither he nor Janet Yellen (a Yale Ph.D.) and Ben Bernanke (an MIT Ph.D.) before him can be called stupid. But how could they be so disconnected from reality? How could they not have learned from the money-printing madmen who came before them? No wonder James Grant complains that the dollar used to be on the gold standard and now it is on the Ph.D. standard.

Grant points out that Powell "does business in a building infused with the doctrines of the hundreds of doctors of economics on the Federal Reserve System's generous payroll." Yet they do not know what the consequences of their actions will be?

Fiddle-de-dee, indeed!

Someone (there is some dispute, but it may have been the great economist Ludwig von Mises) once said that government is the only agency that can take a useful commodity like paper, slap some ink on it, and make it totally worthless.

So, if we wanted to find something kind to say about today's money madmen, we could point out that they have mostly digitized their legalized counterfeiting, reducing the need to lay waste to whole forests as they ramp the money printing to infinity and beyond.

CHAPTER TWO
REAL MONEY –
FREE PEOPLE

Let us start with a few questions.

If you intended to put money into a time capsule for a hundred years or so to leave wealth for some future generation of your family, would it be better to leave them US dollars?

Or gold?

If the State made it illegal for you to own gold, do you think it would be because it was trying to protect you from something secretly dangerous about gold? Or would it be because the State wanted all the gold for itself?

If you woke up living in a police state, is it more likely that the monetary system would be gold? Or would it be some paper or digital money made up by the State?

These questions should all answer themselves, but if they do not, you really need to read this book. And even if you know the answers you need to read this book anyway, because if is about something intangible that is as precious as gold.

That something is freedom.

All the gold mined in human history, around 200,000 tons, is still in human hands. But throughout history freedom has a way of slipping through people's hands. And once lost it is not easily reclaimed.

It is true that freedom has never before had the reach it has now. But if it is not well rooted, it is *always* in danger of being taken away—as new developments continually demonstrate. Freedom is especially vulnerable in a crisis.

The history of money and the history of freedom prove to be closely related. And in fact, it has been observed that you can draw reliable conclusions about the state of freedom in a country when you cross international borders and exchange one currency for another.

But back to our questions.

You would certainly be better off preserving wealth for the future with gold than with dollars or any other government-issued paper money. Indeed, you could leave gold coins at the bottom of the deep blue sea for a thousand years and retrieve them rust free and untarnished. That physical incorruptibility of gold, as it retains its beauty, color, and luster, is a significant corollary with its superiority to corruptible government money. Little wonder, therefore, that gold has endured as money all around the globe for thousands of years, while the history of government money is a history of failure.

Many nation-state currencies have been destroyed by hyperinflation, others by war, replacement, repudiation, and changes in governments.

The value of gold, on the other hand, has never been destroyed by hyperinflation, war, replacement, repudiation, or changes in government. On the contrary no other currency has performed like gold. In his book

The Way the World Works, Jude Wanniski describes gold's exemplary powers of wealth preservation through long sweeps of modern history:

> In England, for example, the wholesale-price index was about 100 in 1717, when Sir Isaac Newton, as Master of the Mint, established the pound sterling in terms of gold. It was still 100 in 1930, giving England more than two centuries of price stability, although there were minor inflations and deflations throughout the long period. During the Napoleonic Wars and during World War I, the government guarantee of paper conversion into gold was suspended, and inflation ensued. But in the post-war periods, when convertibility was reestablished at the prewar ratios, prices also fell until the prewar price levels were reached.
>
> In the United States, the dollar-gold ratio was established in 1792, and except for the Civil War period and briefly during World War I, the dollar remained convertible into gold. The experience with prices was the same as in England. The wholesale-price index was the same in 1930 as it was in 1800. Inflation followed Roosevelt's devaluation of the dollar in 1934, from $20.67 to the ounce to $35; but... the chronic inflation did not begin until the dollar-gold link was finally severed in the seventies.

Sometimes paper money is issued as a receipt for precious metal coins or bullion purportedly held by the State, and exchangeable or redeemable for gold and silver. As you will discover from the American experience, such promises of redeemability soon prove to be hollow.

Certainly, when governments forbid the use of gold it is not because they deem gold to be of no value or somehow dangerous to the health of the people. When the redeemability of the paper money ends, the State ends up keeping the now demonetized gold (and silver) as an act of self-enrichment. As you will discover, less than a hundred years ago the federal government criminalized the ownership of gold by the American people. One should dwell on this: the ownership of gold was a crime against the State in the US, just as it was in Hitler's Germany and in Stalin's Soviet Union. While Washington's plunder of the peoples' gold is a black mark against the State, it does not speak well for the generation of Americans that let the State get away with this rapacious act of tyranny.

Most government money is *fiat* money. "Fiat" in this case does not refer to the Italian auto maker. It is a Latin word meaning "let it be done." It is an imperious order, the kind of thing that kings and emperors toss around. "Fiat money" is only money because the government says it is money. Fiat money is often accompanied by draconian laws and capital punishment to assure that it is used exclusively in the peoples' commerce and that competing forms of money are forbidden. But no government or anyone else ever needs to decree that gold has value.

Gold's value is intrinsic.

To say that gold's value is intrinsic is the same as saying that it is self-evident, just as are the truths Mr. Jefferson referred to in declaring the independence of the American people.

If you woke up in a police state, you would no doubt find that you are living in a monetary system that is exploited to the advantage of the State and to the detriment of the people. As present trends and the latest initiatives show, fiat monetary systems are proving to be especially useful as tools of total State surveillance and control. While fiat money is a tool of the totalist state, Mises points out that real money is among the most important guarantors of the people's freedom:

> It is impossible to grasp the meaning of the idea of sound money if one does not realize that it was devised as an instrument for the protection of civil liberties against despotic inroads on the part of governments. Ideologically it belongs in the same class with political constitutions and bills of right.

Although statists often demean gold, calling it a barbarous relic or only suitable for the construction of public toilets, gold itself does not much care. It need not speak for itself, because throughout history, the people always speak for it. Given a choice between fiat money and gold, people chose gold.

LEGAL TENDER

Few of us would care to the point of insisting that punitive laws be passed if some strange class of our fellow citizens preferred something else to gold; if they should choose to keep and save fiat US money for their old age. It is their business if they persist in placing trust blindly in power-hungry politicians, or if they choose some equally ill-fated currency after the dollar's demise, perhaps some unbacked money substitute from the International Monetary Fund or the World Bank. There are benighted economists who think such multinational bureaucratic contrivances should be the money of the future and should be mandated by governments. If your neighbor were among them, you might try to talk some sense his way, but you probably would not choose to shackle him and throw him in a cage for acting foolishly.

Yet that is exactly what legal tender laws propose to do to people who prefer gold. It is easy to spot fraudulent money schemes; they depend upon force. Criminal laws mandate the use of fiat money and prohibit the usage of competing currencies. That is why Dr. Gono had his thugs arrest and beat people conducting business in something other than Zimbabwe's worthless currency. Courts sometimes refuse to enforce contracts executed in terms other than the State's currency. But it is apparent that societies based on mutual agreement and cooperation rather than on incessant compulsion will prefer real money. No one needs to resort to legal tender laws and the penal code to make people prefer honest money. There is a term for the age-old natural preference people have for sound money. It is called Gresham's law. It states that "bad money drives out good," meaning that people will spend and pass along an inferior money, while holding on to superior money for themselves. When the US government began replacing real silver coins in the 1960s with coins created to mimic silver, people saved the real silver coins, which soon disappeared from circulation while the ersatz silver coins circulated in daily commerce.

GOLD HATERS

Why gold is hated by some is at first glance a mystery: it makes no demands on anyone; it forces its will on no one. It adorns the human body beautifully. Its physical properties of malleability and ductility make it idea for magnificent jewelry and fine works of art. It delights the eye like a rose in full bloom or a morning sunrise.

So why should it be hated? What is it to others if some want to use gold as a medium of exchange or a store of value? In the words Thomas Jefferson used in another context, "It does me no injury... It neither picks my pocket nor breaks my leg."

With this discussion we have begun to suggest why gold is the money of free people. Its usage does not require a multitude of offices or swarms of officers, much less the proliferation of laws and penalties, while fiat money depends on compulsion; as the fiat money moves toward its intrinsic value, the armed power of the State becomes more prominent.

But there is more to it. Gold is hated for the same reason that the burglar hates locks on your doors. For the same reason that looters want to defund the police. It represents a first line of defense against theft. Government can obtain the money it needs, and officials can continue to stovepipe wealth to their crony accomplices with taxation. But that builds resentment because taxation is mostly visible. Inflation is a stealthy means of plundering the people. It is hidden from view.

Mises provides us a compact description of the difference between the government obtaining money through taxation and through inflation, the creation of fiat money by printing or by digital means.

Suppose that a government wants to fight an elective or needless war in some far-off land. The people are bound to weigh any perceived benefit for such a war against the taxes they will have to pay for it. When the government collects the money in taxes to pay for the warships and aircraft, the construction of foreign bases, the manpower and munitions of destruction, the taxpayers footing the bill are forced to restrain their own spending a like amount (which in the case of warfare can be considerable). Individuals accordingly must reduce their own consumption, investment, or savings a like amount.

"The citizen buys less," in such cases, says Mises, "but the government buys more. The government, of course, does not always buy the same goods the citizens would have bought. But on the average there occurs no rise in prices" due to the government's spending.

Suppose, he continues, that without resorting to inflating, the government used "the tax-collected money for hiring new employees or raising the salaries of those who are already in government service. Then these people, whose salaries have been increased, are in a position to buy more. When the government taxes the citizens and uses the money to increase the salaries of government employees, the taxpayers have less to spend, but the government employees have more."

"Prices in general will not increase."

But things are different when the government prints or issues more fiat money. In that case, the recipients of the new money—the beneficiaries of the government spending—will have more, while the rest will have what they had before. "So those who received the newly printed money will be competing with those people who were buyers before. And since there are no more commodities than there were previously, but there is more money on the market—and since there are now people who can buy more today than they could have bought yesterday—there will be an additional demand for that same quantity of goods. Therefore, prices will tend to go up. This cannot be avoided, no matter what the use of this newly issued money will be."

Needless to say, when people feel the sting of taxation, they can express themselves at the ballot box. But, as we have pointed out already and may point out again, inflation is called stealth taxation. Most people, including those in the media who explain arcane things to average Americans at home, have little understanding of how the process works. They tend to believe that price increases are just a natural phenomenon or are a malady that simply appears, like a flu epidemic, instead of a deliberate policy of the State.

Of course, gold short-circuits all these monetary machinations. Like the alchemists of old who could not turn lead into gold, today's central bankers cannot print gold either. Gold provides a discipline on the political classes and their cronies.

On close inspection, then, it is clear that gold is disdained by those want to enrich themselves at the people's expense, by those who want to conceal the costs of their schemes, by those who want to control other people and rob them of their economic freedom. It frustrates the power hungry in their desire to rule others and reward their enablers. As Ron Paul said, "Because gold is honest money it is disliked by dishonest men."

THE WAR ON GOLD

Shortly after the US severed the last link of the dollar to gold in 1971, historian Antony Sutton chronicled "the war on gold" with a book of that name. Sutton wrote that "a totalitarian new world order is likely to be the coming sad fate of a once bright and promising American dream. A society that commenced with libertarian ideas and limited government is degenerating into a totalitarian nightmare, and the war on gold is a necessary device to impose this totalitarian state."

In what sounds very much like anticipation of today's conditions, with the US debt structure close to toppling, the Federal Reserve printing money at a pace that would have been inconceivable just a few short years ago, and central banks around the world beginning to abandon the dollar in favor of gold, Sutton wrote that "at some time in the future, under the pressure of economic events, gold will reassert itself and the establishment elite will have a choice: either adopt the discipline of gold or resort to naked force to impose a paper fiat dollar on both American citizens and the world at large. The history of totalitarian elites suggests that the use of force will be chosen over the right of the people to decide for themselves what they want to use as money."

Sutton concludes that "individual liberty can only be guaranteed under a gold standard with no monopoly power over money issues. That is what the discipline of gold is all about."

History is rich with the tales of lands that have contributed so greatly to the improvement of human life, where people have prospered both economically and in growing freedom around honest precious metal currencies. These are the golden civilizations: Athens, Rome, Byzantium, Florence, Great Britain... and most recently the American Republic.

CHAPTER THREE

THE FREE REPUBLIC IS BORN

It should not need to be said.

But these are times in which statues of their betters are torn down and their memories cursed by squalid mobs of the ignorant who have accomplished nothing with their own lives. It should not need to be said, but a surly and destructive rabble of the ungrateful, bred by a life of entitlements, dominates our high places, our public life, and our discourse, and need to hear it.

So, let it be said. The founders of this country were a gift of the ages to us. They were men of character, learning, accomplishment, and vision.

It is one of the great mysteries of life, and a breathtaking coincidence of history, that when a remarkable group of people appears at one time and in one place, a providential period flourishes because of them. Only barbarians can fail to notice this. In fifth century BC Athens, it was the philosophers Socrates, Plato, and Aristotle, historians Herodotus and

Thucydides, the playwrights Aeschylus, Sophocles, and Euripides, the physician Hippocrates, and many other remarkable souls.

The Florentine Renaissance of the fifteenth century is another such period. Just imagine Leonardo, Botticelli, Donatello, Raphael, and Michelangelo all showing up at around the same time in a town no bigger than Rogers, Arkansas or Casper, Wyoming.

And then there were American colonials of the eighteenth century, the remarkable group consisting of Washington, Franklin, Jefferson, Hamilton, Madison, and John Adams. Without them there is liable to have been no great American Republic. In its place we might have seen a land carved up by European powers with their constant wars and petty interests, kings and potentates vying for power and striving to conquer and rule the continent. But for that remarkable handful of colonials, who knows what European madness might have taken root in the new continent: perhaps the divine right of hereditary monarchs; the Jacobin socialist reign of terror that began at the time the US Constitution was written, turning the streets of France into rivers of blood; something as bad from later Germany; or even a reign of Bolshevism such as Russia endured.

THE REAL REVOLUTION

Instead, our founders did something that had never been achieved before. They stood the old-world order on its head and proclaimed that people are not the pawns or property of the many kings, chieftains, churches, emperors, tyrants, or states.

Always before in the relationships of people and their governments, such rights as people had were assumed to have been conferred upon them by the ruling authority. This was the case even in the signing of the Magna Carta in 1215. The rights that King John was forced to sign over were assumed to have been his to bestow or withhold to begin with.

But the great figures of America's founding saw things differently: all rights reside first with the people, who in turn may bestow some powers upon the State for the accomplishment of specific purposes; or they may withhold those powers from the State.

That was the real revolution the founders accomplished. It was good to be rid of the insane British king and the peacocks of Parliament. But that was secondary to the real revolution.

It is true that each of our founders had shortcomings. We acknowledge, as do all honest human beings, that even as we ourselves have faults, so, too, did they. It is also true that among the founders there are some whose views we prefer, others not as much. But they each made meaningful contributions to the establishment of this new relationship of individual human beings to the State.

It is not just we who say that this generation of American founders were a breed apart. As the gifted historian Paul Johnson writes, "Great events in history are determined by all kinds of factors, but the most important single one is always the quality of the people in charge; and never was this principle more convincingly demonstrated than in the struggle for American Independence."

That the founders prevailed against the mightiest nation on earth was also due in part to the quality of the people they were up against. Although British himself, Johnson does not shrink from an honest appraisal of George III and his retinue. They were "second raters," "boobies," and "a dismal succession of non-entities." In contrast, behind great men like Washington, Jefferson, and Franklin, America had a second rank, and even a third, "solid, sensible, able men capable of rising to great occasion. In personal qualities, there was a difference as deep as the Atlantic between the men who led America during these years, and it told from first to last."

Although the colonies were already at war with the British Empire, the new union of thirteen colonies announced its independence on July 4, 1776. While the Articles of Confederation, which established a new Continental Congress, was ratified in 1781, it was not until the Treaty of Paris was signed in 1783 that the War for Independence officially ended.

But there were problems. Chief among them was one which returns us to our central theme. George Washington identified it in a word: money.

The Continental Congress had issued fiat money, printing it by the wagon load. In fact, Washington complained that "a wagon load of money will scarcely purchase a wagon load of provisions."

The British used the fiat Continental currency regime to conduct economic warfare against the rebels. They counterfeited the Continental dollars in huge numbers to accelerate their depreciation and subvert the American economy. Benjamin Franklin wrote, "The artists they employed performed so well that immense quantities of these counterfeits which issued from the British government in New York, were circulated among the inhabitants of all the states, before the fraud was detected. This operated significantly in depreciating the whole mass."

Another age-old lesson in the difference between real money—gold and silver—and paper money played out right on the stage of the Revolutionary War. The French troops fighting on behalf of the Americans were paid in gold, which they used to purchase goods from American merchants. Americans and their army's agents had nothing but paper money. They noted that the French money drew goods to them from far and wide, ("the people will go through thick and thin" for the French gold) leaving nothing for American agents to purchase.

Nevertheless, one monetary history cites a woman saying at the time, "What a shame it is that Congress should let the poor soldiers suffer, when they have to power to make just as much money as they choose."

Two and a half centuries later, the same sentiments—the State can make all the money it wants—are uttered on behalf of every socialist scheme and pipe dream under the sun by popular political figures like Alexandria Ocasio Cortez and Elizabeth Warren. These would-be Gideon Gonos are boundlessly celebrated by the statist media in direct proportion to their cluelessness.

But unlike today's governing classes, the framers of the Constitution were learned men. They, too, had experienced the "not worth a Continental" sorrows and deprivations of the paper money schemes they had inherited from the sudden amalgamation of thirteen separate colonies.

THE CONSTITUTION

They also knew the historical precedents of freedom won and lost. So, in creating the new Republic, they went to great lengths to protect our freedom. They constrained the power of the new State at every turn. They divided the State's power among the branches. They provided checks on each branch. And the framers made clear in the first ten amendments to the Constitution that the central government could only exercise such powers as it was specifically granted. Instead, they forbid powers to the government beginning with their first five words: "Congress shall make no law…" Other prohibitions follow in series: "the right of the people… shall not be infringed"; "the right of the people… shall not be violated"; "the right… shall be preserved."

Just as they drew up the Constitution with an eye to protecting our freedoms, they sought to protect our wealth. They specifically wrote into the new nation's Constitution a gold- and silver-based monetary system.

First, they gave Congress the power to coin money. From Article I, Section 8, *"Congress shall have Power… to coin Money."*

Not print. Coin.

Since the framers clearly knew the difference, it is hard to believe that proponents of today's irredeemable, unbacked printing-press and digital money schemes can get away with conflating printed money with coined money. Congressional authority to coin money is correspondingly granted in the same clause that tasks Congress with fixing "the Standard of Weights and Measures."

In Section 10 they again addressed the monetary system, again without ambiguity: *"No state… shall make any Thing but gold and silver Coin a Tender in Payment of Debts."*

The deep distrust of paper money was expressed by one delegate to the Constitutional Convention who described any authority for the new government to issue paper money ("to emit bills of credit") as a threat "as alarming as the mark of the Beast in Revelations." His concern was justified. Many of the states had issued such bills of credit. Although they could be used to pay taxes due the issuing state, the bills were not redeemable in gold or silver, and so were bound to depreciate like any other fiat money.

The Articles of Confederation had allowed the national government to "emit bills" as well. It was an inflationary disaster and one of the primary reasons for the failure of the government under the Articles of Confederation. Accordingly, delegates to the Constitutional Convention wanted to use the opportunity to "crush paper money" once and for all. One voiced an opinion shared by many when he said he would rather the Constitution fail than admit a paper money system. In the final vote on the issue only two states approved granting the central government authority to issue paper money; nine states voted against.

The matter was settled.

Nevertheless, we have a paper money system today. Law professor Butler Shaffer once quipped that "the Constitution is that sacred document that prevents the government from doing all the terrible things it does." Despite the framers' best efforts, today gold and silver are nowhere to be found in the State's monetary system. That means that today, not only have the founders been betrayed, you have been betrayed as well. The State no longer protects your wealth.

Today it is up to you to protect your own wealth.

But then, sound money contributed to a booming economy and the spreading of prosperity. But what is there to be surprised about? When money is sound, property is secure and people are free, the human condition improves. Tolerance becomes a norm, culture flourishes, and people become industrious and rich. In his book *One Nation Under Debt*, Robert Wright describes conditions following the adoption of the Constitution:

> "People's incentives changed. Assured that their lives, liberties, and properties were safe, Americans began to invest in the future. The fence that seemed too much trouble to erect in 1785 looked like a necessity in 1789. In 1786, when interest rates were high and real estate values low, repairing the dam and the millrace seemed too expensive. By 1791, with interest rates falling and property values climbing, the repairs would pay for themselves

quickly. Impossible tasks in 1782, like connecting Philadelphia and Lancaster with a good road, were in motion by 1792. In short, the Constitution unleashed the nation's latent entrepreneurial energies....

"When people find it easy to make money hand over fist, they tend to forget about past problems and concentrate instead on the present and future."

The gold and silver standard that the Constitution envisioned functioned admirably until about the time of the creation of the Federal Reserve System in 1913 and the expansion of credit money that financed World War I. Although there were mild inflations and deflations along the way, the new Republic thrived as precious metals produced remarkable stability and confidence in the purchasing power of the dollar. The major exception was the period of the "greenback dollar," unbacked paper money issued during the Civil War. But even the greenback dollars of that period were eventually paid off in gold, dollar for dollar.

DISREGARDING THE CONSTITUTION

In the Federalist Papers, a group of essays urging the people to adopt the proposed Constitution, Alexander Hamilton argued the widely understood general principle that there was no need to prohibit any power to the general government that it had not been expressly granted. No paper money or legal tender authority had been granted, so it could be safely assumed that it had no such authority. Yet the post–Civil War Supreme Court upheld the government's emission of bills that would be legal tender, on the grounds that such authority "was not expressly withheld from Congress by the Constitution."

And that began the reversal of the American Revolution. Recall that it turned on the assertion that all rights are lodged in the people, who in turn empower the State with authority for specific, limited functions. In this way America would be unlike the governments that had gone before. Now the Supreme Court was endorsing government actions not merely because they were "not expressly withheld," but on the grounds that they were "powers belonging to sovereignty in other civilized nations."

The court said that if other governments do it, ours can, too. (See *Juilliard v. Greenman*, 1884.) It was such court decisions—clearly contrived sophistry then as now, and an affront the plain language of the Constitution and intent of the framers—that prepared the way for all the monetary calamities rolling our way.

Long before the street rabble began tearing down the statues, another kind of rabble, the rabble of the governing classes, began tearing down the real contributions of men like Washington, Jefferson, Franklin, and Madison.

We will jump forward to our modern era soon enough. But first, let us look more closely at both gold and silver to discover their qualities and properties and see how they have evolved into ideal money linked to our prosperity and freedom.

CHAPTER FOUR
WHY GOLD?

There is something about gold.

Somebody once quipped that there are two kinds of people: those who "get" gold and those who do not.

Unfortunately, they tend to marry one another.

That is good for a laugh, but it explains nothing. There are remarkable things about the physical properties of gold, things like specific gravity that can be represented with numbers. We will get to those. There are things about gold that make it convenient to serve as money. Some of them have to do with physical properties. We will get to them, too.

But all that will still leave something unsaid about gold. Something that is perhaps only captured in words like "allure." If it were a person, we might choose a word like "charisma" for gold, a word that comes to us out of its religious roots meaning "favor" or "a special spiritual gift from

God." We know people with charisma when we are in their presence, as they often exude a kind of magnetism or special quality.

THE QUALITY OF GOLD

Now we are talking about quality. Ours is an age that tends to devalue quality because it cannot be weighed or measured, as are quantities. Quality is therefore marginalized as "unscientific."

But there is an instrument that is sensitive to quality, and it is curious that it is so easily and perhaps deliberately overlooked: it is our consciousness. That is the only faculty capable of discerning quality. Supreme Court Justice Oliver Wendell Holmes remarked that the universe does not know the difference between champagne and ditchwater. Oh? But we do know. The universe produced us with the potential to be discerning and intelligent. We are very much a part of the universe, the self-conscious part, and we can, and some of us do, know the difference between things high and low, sacred and profane, between champagne and ditchwater.

The Christian writer C. S. Lewis made intellectual sport of people like Holmes, those who reduce everything to its constituent elements, such as turning a da Vinci painting into nothing but so many grams of pigment of this color and that. Lewis called such people "urban blockheads" and "trousered apes." They are stunted in imagination, literalists, and rationalist to a fault. They miss much of the world and life. For lack of quantifiable characteristics, they would prefer to deny the reality of all unmeasurable qualities. The irony is that despite their lopsided consciousness, denying quality all they want, most such men would still be sooner drawn to a beautiful woman than a plain one, without knowing why: that there is something about beauty.

All of this is a long, but important, way of saying that even though the "urban blockheads" call it a barbarous relic and a pet rock, there is something about gold.

While the benighted may not get it about gold's quality, advertisers certainly do. Gold jewelry advertisers have long promoted its irresistibility and captivating qualities to good effect.

The poets, of course, with their odes and rhymes and metaphors and similes, know something about quality, too. The good ones try to capture it: the quality of a moment, a glimpse of nature, a feeling out of the ordinary. When Neil Young sings of searching for "a heart of gold"—an expression that comes from Shakespeare—he is not looking for a meat heart, a literal cardiac muscle, or one made of metal. He is mixing the timeless metaphors, singing about the heart as the center of love, and gold as a symbol of purity and shining incorruptibility. (Indeed, gold's incorruptibility is a polar opposite, a perfect counterpart to government money. Whether made of paper or digital, fiat money is born in corruptibility and issued precisely because it can be corrupted by the issuing authority. But that is getting ahead of our story.)

The mystics have a keen appreciation for gold. Some have called it crystalized sunlight. The ancient alchemists used the same symbol for gold and the sun, a circle with a point in the middle, while the modern chemical symbol for gold, Au, comes from the Latin world for gold, "aurum," which in turn come from the name Aurora, the goddess of the dawn.

Gold's superior nature is honored in our daily usage of term like gold prizes, golden ages, the golden rule, golden mean, and good as gold. In the East gold figures prominently in holy places and sacred occasions: rituals, festivals, and marriages.

Lewis's trousered ape has its opposite extreme also. It is characterized not by the ubiquitous reductionism of our age, but by an inappropriate overvaluation. The myth of King Midas warns of this attitude, for when Midas asked the god Dionysus for the gift of the golden touch, he found that everything he touched, including his food, and in one telling even his daughter, turned to gold. Midas had to implore Dionysus to relieve him of this gift/curse.

The tale even made its way into the James Bond motion picture *Goldfinger*. The song from the film says to beware of the villainous Auric Goldfinger and his Midas touch:

Beware of this heart of gold.

This heart is cold

He loves only gold

Only gold.

THE PROPERTIES OF GOLD

Let us switch now from the mythic and poetic qualities of gold to its physical properties.

Gold is a dense, heavy, soft, and malleable metal. Its color can be described as yellow, but yellow does not do it justice. If you will forgive the tautology, it is more accurately described as the color gold.

Gold is a chemical element with an atomic number of 79. It has a specific gravity of 19.3, which means it weighs 19.3 times more than the same volume of water. That is much heavier than lead, which has a specific gravity of 11.34. Silver and copper are even lighter at 10.49 and 8.95, respectively. At 19.25, tungsten comes close to gold's specific gravity, while uranium is 18.95. Gold's melting point is 1,064 degrees centigrade.

Gold is one of the least reactive chemical elements. Of the "noble" metals (differentiated from the base metals), it is the most noble, resisting corrosion and oxidation like silver and platinum. So resistant to corrosion is it, that when pirated treasures are recovered from the ocean floor after hundreds of years, the gold coins retain the shine and luster they had the day they slipped into the watery depths.

Gold never oxidizes. When the gold coffin of the boy king Tutankhamun was discovered in Egypt in 1922, it and his famous golden mask were perfectly preserved and still stunning to behold despite the passage of more than 3,000 years.

Because of this resistance to corrosion and its high electrical conductivity, gold is used in electrical contacts in high-tech applications. Much of this demand is inelastic, meaning that the demand for gold in these applications changes little when the price moves up. A single mobile phone may use 50 milligrams of gold, only about $3.00 worth at recent prices, which is a small part of the overall cost of the phone. A change in the price of gold is not likely to have much impact on demand for mobile phones.

So great is gold's ductility that a single ounce can be drawn into a wire only a single atom wide, fifty miles in length. A single ounce can be beaten into a thin sheet covering nine square meters, so thin that it becomes partially translucent, transmitting a greenish-blue light. A stack of 7,000 such sheets would be thinner than a dime. Polyester films with gold coating are used in space vehicles and instruments to reflect infrared radiation and to help manage temperatures. The visors of astronauts' helmets are coated with gold for the same reason.

Gold leaf or gold powder is sometimes used as a decorative component of expensive confections and drinks, and consumed. It is non-toxic. Gold's use as a medicine in China dates back at least 4,000 years, as does its appearance in India's ancient ayurvedic medical tradition. Still widely practiced today, ayurvedic medicine includes many gold-based preparations. Gold is also used in modern medicine, specifically in the treatment of arthritis, while radioactive gold is used in cancer treatments. Gold has also been used in dental applications for thousands of years.

A WORLD WITHOUT MONEY

Imagine that you are a soccer coach and in need of dental work. How likely is it that you could find a dentist who just happens to need soccer coaching? And even if you find one, at what rate do you exchange services? How about an hour of coaching for an hour of dentistry? That hardly seems fair, though, because other than a soccer ball and a place to play in a public park, you do not need a lot of extras to be a soccer coach. But a properly equipped dentist has X-ray equipment, drills, special chairs, medicines and anesthesia, filings and amalgams, specialty tools (that must be sanitized to reuse), lights, telephones, dental assistants, staff, and office space. And what about those dental assistants who allow the dentists to work more efficiently? Do they get an hour of soccer coaching for each hour they work on you, too? That hardly seems fair since the dentist has long years of expensive schooling invested in his profession, while his assistant has much less.

Besides, what if a dentist were interested in having you coach his kids in soccer, but you do not happen to need any dentistry? Would he be indebted to you until you get a toothache? Would he be unable to move away or retire until the exchange is settled?

This "double coincidence of wants"—that both parties must have and want to exchange what the other has—is a hurdle for barter that simply cannot be leapt. It quickly becomes apparent what a wonderful thing money is, easily solving this problem and making possible a sophisticated economy, one that cannot survive based on barter. Money enables us exchange with others with whom we need no offsetting transaction. It regularizes prices so that there is not a soccer coaching price of bread and a dental services price of bread and a tire repair price of bread—and untold thousands of other prices for a single good or service.

Money allows us to build for the future. It provides for specialization and efficiency. And most marvelous of all, it allows us to achieve our own needs and desires by serving the needs of others, countless people we may never know or need to meet.

But where did money come from? How did it evolve? Economists of the Austrian school, notables like Mises and Murray Rothbard, explain that with a regression analysis. They look back to the time when a commodity was valued for its own use, theoretically the day before it was used as a unit of exchange. Money developed when individuals began using some otherwise valuable commodity not for present consumption alone, but for saving for real goods and services in the future and for indirect exchange. It was therefore not the artificial creation of a chieftain or king or church or state, but arose through the real-world needs of people to produce, exchange, and thrive.

This brief digression leads us right back to our original question: why gold? After all, many things have been used as money: seashells, loaves of bread, cattle, animal skins, chocolate bars and cigarettes, tree bark inscribed with markings, paper with official-looking insignia and mottos, and even digital bookkeeping entries.

GOLD AS MONEY

The answer is found in an examination of the basic qualities of a reliable money. Here are some qualities of a sound, functional money, characteristics that can be traced back to their recognition by Aristotle 2,400 years ago.

Sound Money Must Be Durable: Because money should be a reliable store of value, gold's durability, its imperviousness to corrosion through centuries and millennia, makes it superior to more perishable forms of money like bread and chocolate bars.

Convenient Money Should Be Portable: Land makes a poor form of money. It suffers from not being portable. Its economic value is also subject to change by natural occurrences and surrounding conditions. Gold is readily portable and substantial worth in gold is commonly moved within countries and around the world.

Reliable Money Must Be Fungible: The value of an acre of land in Manhattan is quite different than an acre of land in the middle of the Mohave Desert. Unlike land, cattle, and animal skins, which can differ greatly in quality and kind, fungibility is a primary feature of gold. Every ounce of pure gold is chemically identical to every other ounce.

Efficient Money Must Be Divisible: The value of a milk cow changes dramatically if it is halved or quartered, while the physical property of gold—its malleability and ductility—makes it readily divisible without loss of value.

Reliable Money Should Be Relatively Scarce: Seashells may lose value in places where more are easily recovered when the tide goes out. The issuance of paper and digital money can be virtually unlimited. But gold is scare. Almost all the gold ever mined throughout history is still in human hands. It is widely disbursed, with almost 70 percent of it held in the form of jewelry and in private hands. If it were all gathered together it would create a cube of just over 71 feet on a side, fitting easily within the bases of a baseball field. This amounts to less than one ounce of gold per person on earth.

All those attributes of sound money are the results of its physical characteristics. But there is one more attribute of sound money:

Money Must Have Intrinsic Value and Be Universally Desirable: Gold is the enduring money of the ages, valued in every corner of the earth. Its innate qualities, discussed at the beginning of this chapter, properties that cannot be weighed or measured but can be recognized by healthy human consciousness—qualities that we have described with terms like allure, charisma, and beauty—make it universally valued and desirable. These are the mythic and poetic qualities of gold that resonate with the deeper levels of human experience. These are qualities that stand in complete contrast to the shabby seals, superficial scrollwork, and bungled manipulation of state money, with all its cheap pretense to value.

There is something about gold.

CHAPTER FIVE
WHY SILVER?

Like gold, there is also something about silver.

Silver has been prized by mankind since before recorded history. It was first mined around 5,000 years ago in Anatolia (modern-day Turkey). Earlier than that, according to legend, ancient shepherds set fire to entire forests for the silver the earth held in its crust. Here is such an account about the inhabitants of the Pyrenees by the Greek historian Diodorus Siculus:

> These Places being full of Woods, and thick of Trees, it is reported that in ancient time this Mountainous Tract was set on Fire by some Shepherds, which continuing burning for many Days together, (whence the Mountains were call'd Pyrenean) the parch'd Superficies of the Earth swet, abundance of Silver and the Ore being melted, the Metal flow'd down in Streams of pure Silver, like a River.

Archaeological digs and burial sites reveal silver used for ornamentation in very ancient times. It was certainly an important component of trade and commerce throughout the ancient Near East, and silver in bulk may have served in a monetary role as far back as 2000 BC. In Genesis 23, Abraham pays 400 "shekels of silver" for a burial site, the first commercial transaction mentioned in the Bible. The payment was not counted out as would have been done with coins, but weighed out in public at the city gates "according to the weight current among the merchants." Proto-coins of precious metals appear to have first been used as currency around 700 BC and soon silver became the first mass-produced coinage.

Even in mankind's early experience with coinage we see examples of the monetary debasement that governments perpetuate to this day. Dionysius I, Greek tyrant of Syracuse whose rule began in 406 BC, was an icon of currency manipulation and debauchery. On one occasion, Aristotle tells us, Dionysius had coins minted of tin and oversaw the passage of a measure commanding that these be accorded the same value as silver coins. Another time, heavily in debt, Dionysius called in all the silver coinage under penalty of death. He then had all the one-drachma coins restamped with the denomination of two drachma. Having doubled the nominal money supply, he returned what he had called in at the new debased face value, and paid debts with the rest. On yet another occasion Dionysius proclaimed that the goddess Demeter had appeared to him, ordering that all the ornaments with which the women adorned themselves be surrendered to the goddess's temple. We do not know whether the women feared Demeter or Dionysius more, but they turned in their valuable jewelry, which Dionysius soon removed to his own treasury.

Despite such incidences, precious metals coinage was such an important development in the advance of commerce and the enrichment of people's daily lives, that silver coinage followed the Greeks all around the Mediterranean region. Since then, silver has been used as money in more places and for longer than gold itself. The Latin word for silver, *argentum*, comes from a proto-Indo-European word meaning "to shine." Argentina gets its name from the Italians who called it *Terra Argentina*, or land of silver.

Argentum is a common root word for money, such as the French *argent*, as are linguistic variations of the English word silver, which is itself derived from Germanic, Norse, and Slavic roots that have echoes in Polish, Russian, and Lithuanian words. The United Kingdom's currency, the pound sterling, evolved from a pound weight of Anglo-Saxon silver coins. The name of the Indian monetary unit, the rupee, comes from a Sanskrit word meaning silver.

THE QUALITY OF SILVER

Like gold, silver has its own mystique. According to the ancient Greek poet Hesiod, the Silver Age of man followed the paradisiacal Golden Age. Although strife entered the world with the Silver Age, it was still one of long life, while war arrived only with the following Bronze Age.

Just as gold is associated with the sun, silver is linked with the moon. The ancient alchemical name for silver is "luna"; its symbol is the crescent moon. In early Greek mythology Selene, the daughter of Titans, is the twin sister of the sun god Helios, and is herself the goddess of the moon. Later in Greece, the moon became associated with Artemis, who was carried across the sky in a chariot pulled by four silver stags and armed with a silver bow from which she fired silver arrows like moonbeams. Fittingly, for a moon goddess, Artemis is also associated with chastity, fertility, and childbirth.

Silver's ability to ward off evil, a property ascribed to it in much of the world, survives in the description of silver's deadly effects on vampires in modern tales, and the effectiveness of silver bullets against werewolves.

Silver is also connected with charming, melodious sounds. It is said that silver "rings true," while everyone recognizes the bright ring of silver bells at Christmas. In *Romeo and Juliet*, Romeo describes lover's soft words as a "silver-sweet" music, while the "silver-tongued" speak words that are seductive and persuasive. Coin collectors know the sound of silver and even have a "ring test," tapping on genuine silver coins to listen for their pure bell-like sound. Try dropping both a US quarter in use today and a real silver quarter minted before 1965 on a hard surface. They may look similar, but it is quite easy to hear the difference. Even though the old quarters are only 90 percent silver, anyone can instantly differentiate their pleasant, clear ringing tone from the dead thump of the base-metal quarters.

THE PROPERTIES OF SILVER

Although silver is described as a brilliant, white metal, its color is better described simply as silver, just as using gold as a descriptive term for gold does its color more justice than the word yellow. Although less so than gold, silver is malleable and ductile, and therefore prized in the manufacture of jewelry, artwork, serving dishes, and dining utensils.

The chemical symbol for silver is Ag, also from *argentum*. Silver is a chemical element with an atomic number of 47. It has a specific gravity of 10.49, which is lighter than lead, but heavier than copper, and a melting point of 961.9 degrees centigrade, about 100 degrees below that of gold.

Silver was employed for its antibacterial properties long before bacteria were discovered in 1676. The Phoenicians stored water, wine, and vinegar in silver bottles to prevent contamination. Similarly, cowboys in the old American west would toss a silver dollar in a barrel of water to keep it safe for drinking. Today silver continues to be used in water purification systems. Hippocrates wrote about silver's use in treating wounds. Because of its antimicrobial properties, silver foil was used to wrap wounds in World War I. This antibacterial property has silver used in a growing number of medical applications today and is the focus of substantial new research in anticipation of the proliferation of bacteria strains resistant to antibiotics due to their promiscuous use. Bacteria do not develop a progressive resistance to silver.

Silver's thermal conductivity is the highest of any metal. It serves as a catalyst in the production of essential industrial chemicals. It is a superior conductor of electricity, although used less often in general applications than copper, which is less expensive, while gold's superior resistance to corrosion makes it suitable for specific higher-performance but higher-cost usages. Silver is a crucial component of digital age products, ubiquitous in circuit boards, microelectronics, and TV screens.

Just as the moon reflects the light of the sun, reflectivity is an important feature of silver. It is the most light-reflective element, reflecting 95 percent of the visible spectrum. Silver discs were used as mirrors in Egypt 4,000 years ago, while silver mirrors were so popular in the Roman Empire that one historian thought to mention "that they began to be used even by maid servants." Today the twin 8.1-meter diameter reflecting primary mirrors of the large ground-based Gemini Observatories in Chile and Hawaii are silver-coated.

A generation ago books on silver investing went on at length about silver's indispensability in photographic applications, including in X-rays. Eastman Kodak, the camera and film company, was the world's largest user of silver forty years ago. Today that demand has shrunk dramatically, as film has progressively been replaced by digital photography. (As a sidebar to our story, Eastman Kodak invented the first digital camera in 1975, but did not exploit the technology for fear it would cannibalize its film business. It was not a wise decision. Eastman Kodak was dropped from the S&P 500 in 2010; it filed for bankruptcy protection in 2012.)

Thanks to silver's photovoltaic properties, it plays an important role in solar energy technology. There is much to be said for analysts who expect that "green" political initiatives will drive new industrial silver demand for solar power applications.

But our focus is elsewhere. Silver demand has a foot in two camps: industrial (including fabrication for jewelry and silverware) and monetary. Industrial applications account for 60 percent of the annual demand of silver production (compared to nine percent of gold's), so industrial demand does move the price of silver. But the big price moves of major bull markets come with a reawakening appreciation for silver's monetary qualities.

SILVER AS MONEY

Silver shares in the monetary qualities of gold discussed in the previous chapter.

Silver Is Durable. Unlike most other commodities, silver is a lasting store of value that is non-perishable and resists corrosion.

Silver Is Portable. While an ounce of gold is many times the value of an ounce of silver (a point that we will discuss in more detail later), silver is sufficiently valuable that an easily carried or movable quantity can function in many day-to-day transactions.

Silver Is Fungible. Every ounce of silver is chemically identical to every other ounce of silver, unlike many historical money substitutes, from livestock to precious stones.

Silver Is Divisible. Coins and bars of varying weights and sizes can be minted with no loss of essential value.

Although more plentiful than gold, silver is relatively scarce. The earth's silver deposits are estimated to be 19 times those of gold. Another estimate suggests that all the silver in transparent industrial and government stockpiles and commodity fund vaults around the world (not including jewelry, silverware, and coins and bullion in private hands) amounts to 3 billion ounces. For a global population approaching 8 billion people, that amounts to 3/8 of an ounce apiece. That is close to the amount of silver in a pre-1965 US fifty-cent coin.

Silver Has Intrinsic Value; It Is Universally Desirable. It has been valued and desired by human beings in every developed civilization virtually everywhere on earth for millennia. As with gold, healthy human consciousness recognizes something of silver's innate quality. The State goes to great lengths to costume its deceitful coinage of base metals to look like, and in a pretense of being the equivalent of, real silver. No matter how many laws it passes, it fails to achieve an equivalency. The monetary flimflammers only ape silver's natural beauty, mystique, and refined quality.

That is because there is something about silver.

There is more to be said about the relative monetary values of gold and silver through history. That discussion is available in Appendix I: GOLD VS. SILVER at the end of the book. But for now, having explored the qualities and properties of both silver and gold, it is time to return to our account of the American experience with real money for free people. The next chapter addresses the most destructive force in America's monetary affairs. One writer calls it the Creature from Jekyll Island. Another refers to the people that run it as the Deep State Money Manipulators.

You know it as the Federal Reserve System.

CHAPTER SIX

THE FEDERAL RESERVE

My choice for the best internet image of the year 2020 is one that crossed my screen just when we most needed a laugh. In a year of floods, fires, earthquakes, killer hornets, and rolling blackouts, to say nothing of the coronavirus and lockdown, unemployment, riots, looting, and arson, someone sent around a picture of Doc Brown from the motion picture *Back to the Future.* Standing next to his time-traveling DeLorean automobile, Doc says to his young friend, "Marty! Whatever you do, don't go to 2020!"

It might have been good if America could have skipped a few things in the year 1913 as well. It was not a good year for our freedom and prosperity. Woodrow Wilson became president that year. His most lasting achievement was inveigling the United States into participating in the slaughter that was World War I. That year also saw the passage of the Sixteenth Amendment, creating the income tax. Opponents arguing against the adoption of that amendment warned that if we were not careful, income taxes might rise to as high as 10 percent. They were off by a factor of nine. The top US marginal tax rate eventually climbed past 90 percent.

1913 was the year the Seventeenth Amendment was added to the Constitution. It provided for the direct election of US senators. This was a power-centralizing move by Washington, the practical result of which was to subordinate the prerogatives of the states and eliminate an important check on the growth of the federal government.

But the most destructive political measure of 1913 was the passage of the Federal Reserve Act establishing a "central bank" for the United States.

We do run into those who do not get our beef with the Federal Reserve. We understand. It would be good if we could simply point out that the creation of the Fed represents a major achievement of Karl Marx's *Communist Manifesto*. In his words "the centralization of credit in the hands of the state, by means of a national bank with state capital and an exclusive monopoly" is one of the ten steps essential to the creation of a communist state. So, unless we want to keep heading down the soul-destroying path of grinding poverty and the eruption of occasional mass starvation and widespread State slavery that millions have experienced under communist rule in places like the Soviet Union, Pol Pot's Cambodia, Mao's China, and North Korea, we should not have created a monetary politburo.

But we do not get off that easily. Most people need more explanation. Although money is a major part of people's lives every single day, few give much thought to what it is and where it comes from. An example of their confusion can be found in an independent survey of Americans in 2019 that found that:

- 29 percent of respondents think the US dollar is still backed by gold. Four percent think the dollar is backed by oil.

- 54 percent think the Federal Reserve is owned by the US government.

- 26 percent think that banks keep on hand 100 percent of their customers' deposits.

Of course, none of these things is true. So, let us start at the beginning by looking at some descriptions of the Federal Reserve System and its activities, starting with the Fed's self-description.

The Fed's website says, "The Federal Reserve, the central bank of the United States, provides the nation with a safe, flexible, and stable monetary and financial system." Among its general functions that we are concerned with in this book, the Fed says it does these things:

- conducts the nation's monetary policy to promote maximum employment, stable prices, and moderate long-term interest rates in the U.S. economy.

- promotes the stability of the financial system and seeks to minimize and contain systemic risks through active monitoring and engagement in the U.S. and abroad.

THE CREATURE FROM JEKYLL ISLAND

But the record will show that the Fed has failed to achieve these objectives. That should not be surprising, because according to G. Edward Griffin, those were not the real objectives of the creators of the Federal Reserve System. Griffin is the author of *The Creature from Jekyll Island*, the definitive history of the creation of the Fed. It details all the interests and machinations that were at work at a secret meeting in 1910 held "at the private resort of J. P. Morgan on Jekyll Island off the cost of Georgia."

> Those who attended represented the great financial institutions of Wall Street and, indirectly, Europe as well. The reason for secrecy was simple. Had it been known that rival factions of the banking community had joined together, the public would have been alerted to the possibility that the bankers were plotting an agreement in restraint of trade—which, of course, is exactly what they were doing.

> What emerged was a cartel agreement with five objectives: stop the growing competition from the nation's newer banks; obtain a franchise to create money out of nothing for the purpose of lending; get control of the reserves of all banks so that the more reckless ones would not be exposed to currency drains and bank runs; get the taxpayers to pick up the cartel's inevitable losses, and convince congress that the purpose was to protect the public.

In terms of those five objectives, says Griffin, the Fed has been an unqualified success.

It is irresponsible for the people to think that the Federal Reserve was designed for anything other than to serve the interests of the banking cartel that created it in the first place; that the banks that borrow from the Fed for a mere 0.25 percent and charge you 15 percent on your credit card are practicing philanthropy; that the Fed that bailed the banks out from their own recklessness during the mortgage meltdown, while millions of Americans lost their homes, was really involved in acts of impartial regulatory oversight.

Economists even have a term for the ubiquitous practice of government boards, bodies, and bureaucrats quietly serving the interests of the industries they are believed to be regulating rather than in the so-called public interest. It is called "regulatory capture."

You do not have to look hard so see that regulatory capture is everywhere. It is at work in the government bodies that regulate high-tech companies, medicine, insurance, pharmaceuticals, telecommunications, transportation, agriculture, housing, and more. One source defines regulatory capture as "a failure of normal government functions." Whether it is the failure or the fulfillment of government functions should be debated. But the Fed is not an agency that was captured by-and-by. It was conceived in the womb of the banking cartel from the very beginning.

So, what does the Fed actually do? It interferes in everything that involves money. It interferes in every business exchange, purchase, or sale and every act of spending or saving money. That is, unless you are a Thoreau living entirely off the grid without ever resorting to the use of money, it interferes in everything. Even then you still cannot escape since you will have to resort to the monetary system to pay taxes on your Walden Pond getaway. (You never really own your property in America today; you only rent it. And if you do not pay your rent-tax, your property will be taken from you.)

The Fed is an invisible partner in every commercial transaction in the land. It performs this function by controlling the conditions of money and credit.

Its activities go by many names. Money pumping. Liquidity operations. Open Market Committee interventions. Quantitative easing. Market stimulation. Interest rate policy. Adding reserves. Demand management. Monetizing the debt. Fine-tuning the economy. Easing credit conditions.

We prefer to call it all "money printing," even when it just does so digitally instead of the old-fashioned way with paper and ink. The Fed is like the proverbial nutjob that finds himself holding a hammer and discovers everything looks like a nail. Just like Havenstein and Gideon Gono that we discussed in Chapter One. The Fed's hammer is the artificial expansion of money and credit. Juicing the markets. Printing money. By any name, the Fed devalues the purchasing power of the dollar and wields a hammer of destruction wherever it goes.

Here is the basic shell game. The Fed creates money by buying financial assets such as US Treasury bonds. Well, it used to be mostly US Treasuries. Lately, in a sign of its desperation, the Fed has been buying financial instruments of increasingly compromised quality, like toxic mortgage securities, corporate bonds, state and municipal bonds, exchange traded funds, and even junk bond funds.

It buys them from a broker, for example a government bond dealer, paying for them with money it does not really have. The bond dealer gets a check from the Fed which it in turn deposits with its bank. The bank then makes a deposit with the Fed, and in our fractional reserve banking system, by virtue of that deposit and the creation of "reserves" with the Fed, the bank is now empowered to make new loans many times greater than the amount of those reserves. It is a magical act of monetary expansion. Fed asset purchases mushroom the amount of money in the economy. In this way, the Fed increases the money supply. If it wants to influence interest rates downward, something it has been doing for most of the last forty years, it will create a lot more money by buying more assets with money it made up out of thin air.

There are a couple of additional twists, things like changing the level of reserves that banks have been required to keep with the Fed (something that is undergoing substantial change as we write, another sign of desperation), or adjusting the discount rate—the rate the Fed charges member banks that borrow from it.

In a healthy economy, prices of things (including interest rates, which are the prices of money) are set by supply and demand. This alleviates shortages and prevents surpluses, helps businesses prioritize production and compare resources, and enables consumers to make informed choices about real costs, spending, and savings.

But the Fed pretends that it can do better. And so, with each interest rate intervention it distorts people's perception of reality. For example, in the Fed's housing bubble artificially low interest rates convinced home-builders that there was much more real demand for housing and ability to meet mortgage payments that there actually was. The Fed sent false signals to the economy. It deluded market participants, both creditors and borrowers. When the bubble burst, 500 banks went under; nearly ten million Americans lost their homes.

That is some destructive hammering.

Most outrageous is the way the Fed dresses all this up as though there is something scientific about what it does. The Fed is awash in high-priced economists and expensive consultants who gather a never-ending flood of statistics.

Still, for all the academic pretense, there is nothing scientific about what the Fed does. No board or body argues about the freezing or boiling point of water, 32 degrees and 212 degrees Fahrenheit, respectively. That is science. In electronics, Ohm's law is science. In chemistry, the periodic table of elements. In astronomy, Kepler's laws.

But the Fed just apes the language of the physical sciences and makes up money supply and interest rate policy to serve favorite constituents, like Wall Street, money center banks, or powerful politicians.

What about the virtues that the Fed's website boasts? The ones about "the stability of the financial system" and "contain[ing] systemic risks." The "safe, flexible, and stable monetary and financial system" that it "provides the nation."

THE DEEP STATE
MONEY MANIPULATORS

What is the Federal Reserve's actual track record?

It could not be much worse. My friend and bestselling author Charles Goyette, who calls the Fed "the Deep State Money Manipulators," sums up the Fed's accomplishments this way in his new book *The Last Gold Rush... Ever!*:

> An endless sequence of booms and busts; the Great Depression and its prolongation; the stagflation decade of the 1970s; the wild whipsawing of interest rates that climbed to as high as 21 percent and were later forced to flirt with zero percent, the latest policy that has created an unwholesome risk tolerance on the part of retirees looking for a return on their lifetime savings; the 1981–1982 recession, which was the worst downturn since the Great Depression, followed by another downturn even worse than the one before, the 2008 Great Recession; record waves of bank failures; millions of Americans losing their homes; the shifting of wealth from the poor and the middle class to the wealthy; and, the bailouts and therefore the perpetuation of badly managed banks.
>
> Meanwhile, the Fed has been indifferent to the dual mandate given it by Congress: maximum employment and price stability. Instead, the Fed has been targeting a 2 percent inflation rate as a policy objective. At that rate, a saver's $50,000 turns into about $30,000 in purchasing power in twenty-five years. And in a quintessential act of the Deep State, during the mortgage meltdown of 2007 and 2008, while Americans were losing their jobs and homes, the Fed loaned more than $16 trillion at the expense of the American people and the risked solvency of the US to foreign central banks and politically connected private banks and companies—even to foreign companies. It desperately tried to keep its financial chicanery concealed from the people.

But the single most destructive practice of the Federal Reserve, a power from which the Deep State derives its financial muscle, is the deliberate shrinking of the dollar's value. Since its inception, the Fed has destroyed 96 percent of the dollar's purchasing power. It does so because, like any inflator or currency counterfeiter, the Deep State derives much of its wealth and power from this practice.

No wonder the Deep State does not want you to own gold.

The long list of Fed failures will eventually prove its undoing and, without the passage of any measures, without mandates, compulsion, or legal tender laws, precious metals will again be central to the monetary system. Then, amid the ruins, people will look back and wonder how the Fed ever crossed its existential bridge. How did it manage to come into being when it is so clearly unconstitutional? The US government is one of enumerated powers. See Article I, Section 8 of the Constitution that details the limited and specific powers of Congress. As we discussed in Chapter Three, it includes the words *"Congress shall have Power... to coin Money."* But nowhere does the Constitution enumerate any congressional authority to create a private banking cartel, or a central bank of any kind, to manage a monetary monopoly or to issue a fiat currency as legal tender. To make the case even more airtight, the Bill of Rights wagged its finger at the central government, ending with the Tenth Amendment's warning that the federal government has only those powers expressly granted to it. Other powers "are reserved to the States respectively, or to the people."

Mises understood that there are no limits on what governments will do to replace the discipline and impartiality of the gold standard with contrivances like the Federal Reserve and the right to issue unbacked money:

> The whole grim apparatus of oppression and coercion—policemen, customs guards, penal courts, prisons, in some countries even executioners—had to be put into action in order to destroy the gold standard. Solemn pledges were broken, retroactive laws were promulgated, provisions of constitutions and bills of rights were openly defied. And hosts of servile writers praised what the governments had done and hailed the dawn of the fiat-money millennium.

CORNERING THE ECONOMICS PROFESSION

If the Constitution were to be openly defied, members of the banking cartel would have to make generous contributions to academia and the burgeoning field of economics to see the Federal Reserve Act passed. Noting that bankers themselves were not likely to persuade the people that their Jekyll Island plans were merely "reforms"—pure expertise entirely detached from all self-interest—Griffin describes in some detail the millions of dollars that the cartel stovepiped to academics who would do the work for them. He quotes economist John Kenneth Galbraith saying, "It is at least possible that the reverence for which the Federal Reserve System has since been held by economists owes something to the circumstance that so many who pioneered in the profession participated in its [the System's] birth."

Enlisting the economics profession to mobilize public opinion was an effective strategy for the banking monopoly. It has sustained Fed apologists, subsidized their overt hostility to gold, and enforced the lockstep Keynesian interventionism in the economics profession ever since. It explains how the economics profession can overlook bubble after bubble, telling us only after the damage has been done that the Fed rode to our rescue and saved the day.

> The Federal Reserve, through its extensive network of consultants, visiting scholars, alumni and staff economists, so thoroughly dominates the field of economics that real criticism of the central bank has become a career liability for members of the profession....
>
> This dominance helps explain how, even after the Fed failed to foresee the greatest economic collapse since the Great Depression, the central bank has largely escaped criticism from academic economists. In the Fed's thrall, the economists missed it, too.

That is from a 2011 Huffington Post investigation by reporter Ryan Grim, "Priceless: How the Federal Reserve Bought the Economics Profession," which uncovered the central bank's continuing outsized influence in the profession. The report details the economists numbering in the hundreds that work for the Fed and the hundreds more that receive study contracts from it at a cost of millions of dollars. The story is also told in the numbers of editorial board members of the leading academic journals who are associated with the Fed, while "affiliations with the Fed have become the oxygen of academic life for monetary economists."

Once brought to life, the creature has proven impossible to control. Some of the smallest businesses in America are audited. The government requires every public company to provide it with audited financial statements. Their CEOs and CFOs must certify and sign those filings. But the Fed, the mother of all regulators, cannot be made to submit to an audit. If you need to be persuaded that Washington is a land of hypocrites, you should find what follows helpful.

In 2010, Congressman Ron Paul's bill to audit the Federal Reserve had 320 sponsors in the House of Representatives. It was no surprise that it had so many sponsors that year. Their constituents were losing their homes and jobs right and left, while even casual observers could see that the Fed's Wall Street cronies were getting bailed out from the latest Fed-created market collapse. College students and ordinary people, showing up wherever Congressman Paul spoke, had taken to chanting "End the Fed! End the Fed!"

So, the Audit the Fed bill had a lot of sponsors. But when the vote finally came up, it only received 198 votes. It failed to pass.

Sponsors voted against their own bill. The Fed, said Dr. Paul afterwards, "is a very powerful institution." Dripping with the effluent of its crony swamp, the Creature from Jekyll Island had gone to work and stopped the measure dead in its tracks.

And as mentioned, it was during that same Great Recession, while Americans were losing their homes and savings, that the Fed was secretly loaning money to many of the financial institutions that were responsible for the calamity, some of the largest and most powerful banks and financial institutions in the world, *including foreign banks and governments.*

No wonder Fed officials so desperately resist an audit. They are the Deep State Money Manipulators. With the creation of the Fed, the banking cartel established a banking monopoly, a franchise for the expansion of its lending base, a means of having the taxpayers backstop its losses, and a fiat currency management system, all cloaked as a disinterested and sophisticated benevolence.

But there remained one obstacle to their total control of money and credit:

Gold.

In the next two chapters you will learn what they were willing to do to deprive free people of real money.

CHAPTER SEVEN
STEALING THE PEOPLE'S GOLD

The journalist and cultural critic H. L. Mencken said that every decent man is ashamed of the government he lives under.

For those in want of justification for that shame, the brazen State theft and fraud described in this chapter and the next should help.

The new Federal Reserve appeared on the scene just in time to help pay for World War I with a massive credit expansion. The lion's share of the war costs was paid for by inflation rather than taxation. Never mind that consumer prices for Americans doubled as a result, amounting to nothing less than a stealth war tax for a war the people did not want. Thanks to the fractional reserve banking system, the Fed's wartime credit expansion continued after Armistice Day. The money supply exploded, up 55 percent between July 1921 and July 1929. It was like an afterburner driving real estate prices higher and creating a fantastic speculative boom in stock prices.

Eventually, like all bubbles, the Fed bubble of the 1920s popped. As everyone knows, stock prices collapsed in October 1929. They soon fell to one-tenth their previous high. Businesses failed, jobs disappeared, consumer spending dried up as disposable incomes fell.

And with that the Great Depression was underway.

HOOVER THE INTERVENTIONIST

The pain was so great and long-lasting because Herbert Hoover, that laissez-faire paragon and misguided devotee of free markets, refused to intervene with the robust measures that Roosevelt eventually implemented.

At least that is what your teachers and textbooks likely taught you. It is what my teachers taught me. And it is what their teachers taught them. Never mind that it is no more true than Bush's assertions about WMDs in Iraq or the Gulf of Tonkin incident that was the pretext for the Vietnam War.

In reality, Hoover, that supposed hard-hearted conservative, did not slash spending, as is so often taught; both spending and the deficits rose sharply on his watch. Between 1929 and 1932 spending jumped almost 50 percent. The 1931 deficit was more than 50 percent higher than the one in 1929. Contrary to the myths, Hoover raised taxes and tax rates on the struggling economy. His high-wage policy, enforced by both legislation and the bully pulpit, meant that salaries were maintained even as the cost of goods and service fell. The net result was that "real wages" rose for those who were still employed, but it was at the expense of the unemployed because businesses hired fewer workers. Inflated salaries exacerbated unemployment and impeded businesses struggling to return to profitability.

To make things worse, Hoover signed the Smoot-Hawley Tariff law in the middle of 1930. Exports plummeted. The unemployment rate jumped from 3.2 percent in 1929 to 8.7 percent in 1930. But that was only the beginning.

Hoover not only signed the biggest tariff bill in history, he also signed into law an increase in the income tax. In *The Way the World Works*, Jude Wanniski wrote, "Most one-term Presidents only have time for one truly disastrous decision, but Hoover squeezed in two."

Some noninterventionist!

In the presidential campaign of 1932, Roosevelt pounded Hoover for his spending, taxing, and for bloating the budget—"the greatest spending administration in peacetime in all of history." Roosevelt's critique was both correct (about the Hoover's policies) and characteristically dishonest (about his own intentions). Between 1933 and 1936, under President Roosevelt, government expenditures climbed by 83 percent; federal debt rose by 73 percent.

The schools need to revise their curricula. Hoover did not fail to intervene in the economy. The country would have suffered less if he had. Indeed, it would have recovered quickly, just as it had a decade earlier.

THE DEPRESSION OF 1920

It is always helpful to look back at the Depression of 1920-21.

Wait!

What depression is that? It is the one that nobody remembers, even though it had all the makings of the Great Depression. Farm prices and wholesale prices fell by more than a third, while the unemployment rate leaped to 15.3 percent. Industrial production fell 30 percent between 1920 and 1921, while stocks prices fell in half.

Conditions were worse than they were after the first year of the Great Depression. But without the guidance of either a Hoover or a Roosevelt, by 1921 the economy had begun a rapid and robust recovery. James Grant, the author of *The Forgotten Depression*, calls the 1920-21 episode "the depression that healed itself."

Well, of course it did. When a bubble has formed, it will pop. It is a reaction to excess. We all know that when things get too far out of whack, they will revert to the mean. When the stock market is inflated in a money-printing mania beyond what the old parameters of real values, prices, and earnings suggest, it will adjust. There is a reason it is called a "correction." But the correction must be allowed to correct.

Here is a rule of thumb you will find helpful. Invariably governments attempt to inflate the economy. The market attempts to restore reality, deflating the malinvestment, but governments do not want to let that happen. It is an old cycle. And so, it was typical that the interventionists Hoover and Roosevelt both refused to let all the malinvestments liquidate and the economy correct. Instead, they burdened the economy further and thus dragged the pain and suffering out for many years, as G. Edward Griffin explains:

> In 1931 fresh money was pumped into the economy to restart the cycle, but this time the rocket would not lift off. The dead weight of new bureaucracies and government regulations and subsidies and taxes and welfare benefits and deficit spending and tinkering with prices had kept it on the launching pad.
>
> Eventually, the productive foundation of the country also began to crumble under the weight. Taxes and regulatory agencies forced companies out of business. Those that remained had to curtail production. Unemployment began to spread. By every economic measure, the economy was no better or worse in 1939 than it was in 1930 when the rescue began.

It makes no difference to the economy if it is loaded with Republican dead weight or Democrat dead weight. In fact, the Hoover-Roosevelt interventionism was a continuum of dead weight. Historian Paul Johnson writes in *Modern Times* that "Roosevelt's legislation, for the most part, extended or tinkered with Hoover's policies." Rather than to wade into the alphabet soup of agencies and acts that Johnson provides as evidence of this continuum, we will just cite, as Johnson does, syndicated columnist Walter Lippman who wrote in 1935: "The policy initiated by President Hoover in the autumn of 1929 was something utterly unprecedented in American history. The national government undertook to make the whole economic order operate prosperously... the Roosevelt measures are a continuous evolution of the Hoover measures."

FDR AND HIGHER PRICES

Instead of seeing low prices as a consequential and an inevitable deflation of the unsustainable prior bubble, a reflection of the real conditions of supply and demand, and thus the antidote the economy needed, Roosevelt, like Hoover, thought it was his job to drive prices up. So, Roosevelt had perfectly good farm crops plowed under. And he had baby piglets and sows, millions of them, slaughtered. This policy madness took place as people were going hungry and desperately needed lower prices to keep their families fed! Roosevelt's administration paid for these outrages with tax dollars it got from the self-same beleaguered people that needed lower prices. The administration spent $31 million on its pig slaughter in 1933. That would be $618 million today.

While it was clear that the economy needed lower prices to wring out prior excesses, and while the people in their reduced circumstances needed lower prices, Roosevelt thought otherwise. Devaluing the dollar was an article of faith with him, even though the outcome of the policy would be that the few dollars the impoverished people had would buy them less and less.

There is always need for another book exploding the big government myths about the Great Depression and the "heroic" Franklin Roosevelt, whose actions deepened and prolonged the economic crisis. But because our objective is to help you prepare for the new depression the statists have engineered, the one that is unfolding right now, having led you to Roosevelt's desire to devalue the dollar, we will have to leave our backstory there and pick up with Roosevelt's grand theft.

THE GREAT GOLD GRAB

It starts in the first days of his presidency, still early in the Great Depression, but before he had a chance to try to pack the Supreme Court, overturn the precedent of presidents limiting themselves to two terms, or provoke a war with Japan and conceal advance warnings the US had about the Japanese attack on Pearl Harbor. And it was long before Roosevelt turned eastern Europe over to the murderous Josef Stalin.

All that would come later. After he had stolen the people's gold. Before Roosevelt's inauguration many people anticipated he would confiscate their gold and debauch the dollar, despite the Democratic party's 1932 platform and Roosevelt's pledge to defend the gold standard. So even before his election those who viewed the government with due suspicion began exchanging dollars for gold (US gold reserves quickly fell, somewhere in the order of 11 million ounces due to those exchanges) and they began exporting their gold for foreign storage or simply hiding it away.

Roosevelt was elected in a landslide on November 8, 1932. He was inaugurated on March 4, 1933.

On March 6, the new president ordered a nationwide "bank holiday." During the closure, banks were forbidden to pay out any gold or engage in foreign exchange. Four days later, on March 10, Roosevelt issued another order extending the gold and foreign exchange prohibitions, except for those who had obtained a special government license.

On April 5, the President issued yet another decree, this one outlawing "hoarding," and confiscating the American people's gold. Among the limited exceptions to Executive Order 6102 was gold for industrial purposes, art, and rare-coin collections. Otherwise, the American people were mostly forbidden to own monetary gold. They were ordered to surrender gold coins, gold bullion, and gold certificates to the Federal Reserve at the prevailing price of $20.67 an ounce (where it had been for a century) "under penalty of $10,000 fine or ten years' imprisonment or both."

The order began by invoking authority under law, including the Trading with the Enemy Act of 1917. America was not at war at the time, so there was no enemy as defined by the Constitution (Article 1, Section gives Congress the sole power to declare war, America's last eighty years of undeclared wars notwithstanding; there is no means other than a war declaration for the designation of an enemy. That is an important protection of the people, as it prohibits politicians from unilaterally and promiscuously declaring "enemies.") Because the Trading with the Enemies Act only empowered the president to restrict trade with its enemies in time of war, the administration had already had Congress extend that authority to peacetime with its Emergency Banking Act, which was passed a few days after Roosevelt's inauguration.

The executive order then proclaimed a national emergency:

> ... I, Franklin D. Roosevelt, President of the United States of America, do declare that said national emergency still continues to exist and pursuant to said section do hereby prohibit the hoarding of gold coin, gold bullion, and gold certificates within the continental United States by individuals, partnerships, associations and corporations.

It concluded by prescribing penalties:

> Whoever willfully violates any provision of this Executive Order or of these regulations or of any rule, regulation or license issued thereunder may be fined not more than $10,000, or, if a natural person, may be imprisoned for not more than ten years, or both; and any officer, director, or agent of any corporation who knowingly participates in any such violation may be punished by a like fine, imprisonment, or both.

On April 18 Roosevelt halted the export of gold. A farm relief bill passed on May 12 included an amendment that allowed the president to change the dollar-gold price.

Congress got into the act on June 5 with a resolution that abrogated both government and private gold contacts. It is worth lingering on this for a moment because the move was a frontal assault on the right to contract. Seeking to protect themselves from a long history of governmental monetary usurpations and abuse, many citizens sought the assurance of entering contracts that specified the party's obligations in terms of specified weights of gold instead of just dollar amounts. As long as $20.67 remained the gold price, contracts could still be settled in the convenience of dollars without one party being fleeced by receiving payment in dollars of reduced value. But the new measure nullified those agreements, allowing debtors including the federal government to ignore the obligations, and paying creditors in cheaper, devalued dollars only. It was a windfall not just for private debtors, but for the federal government. The result was that creditors who had gold contracts were swindled by $3 billion, about $78.5 billion in today's dollars. Conscientious individuals who had taken measures that were both prudent and common at the time were forced to accept payment in the new and capriciously established value of the dollar.

To say the value of the dollar became capricious with Roosevelt's intervention is no overstatement. In his diary, Secretary of the Treasury Henry Morgenthau described discussing the gold price in the White House as the president enjoyed breakfast in bed. Roosevelt arbitrarily ordered a 21-cent price increase that day. His economic rationale? "It is a lucky number," the president laughed, "because its three times seven." Morgenthau wrote in his diary, "If anybody ever knew how we really set the gold price through a combination of lucky numbers, I think they would be frightened."

Outlawing gold contracts and criminalizing gold ownership was not the end of it. On January 30, 1934, the Gold Reserve Act passed. It lodged title to all gold coins and bullion in the federal government. (The US gold depository at Fort Knox, Kentucky, was built to accommodate the new reserves that had been seized from the people and the flow of gold from abroad.) The act also permitted the president to set a new dollar gold price, which Roosevelt did the following day. The new gold price, he proclaimed, was $35 an ounce.

This was an act of massive dollar devaluation. The gold content of the dollar was diluted by 41 percent.

Not everyone supported the gold theft. Senator Carter Glass, remembered today for the Glass-Steagall Banking Act, called it "dishonorable." Another senator, the grandfather of the late author Gore Vidal, called the gold grab what it was, as Mises Institute senior fellow Ralph Raico relates:

> One of the last holdouts was another "reactionary," Thomas P. Gore, Democrat of Oklahoma, who, though blind, was one of the most learned men in the U.S. Senate. When FDR asked him

what he thought of the new policy, Gore replied: "Well, that's just plain stealing, isn't it, Mr. President."

Roosevelt never forgave Gore, who committed the added sin, from the president's standpoint, of being a confirmed "isolationist" in foreign affairs.

Here at the end of this chapter, two questions remain: Why did he do it? And how did he get away with it?

Let us take the second question first. How did Roosevelt and his myrmidons get away with it? Serious students of history will quickly discover that Roosevelt and this "brain trust" of statists, collectivists, socialists, and more than a few communists and economic imbeciles (although I repeat myself) got away with a lot of things. How did they get away with enacting Mussolini socialism in the US? How did they get away with dragging out the Great Depression for so long? And to refocus on our specific issue, how did they get away with stealing the peoples' gold?

A fair share of the blame must land in the lap of the American people.

Article VI, Clause 3 of the Constitution requires that US senators and representatives, as well as state legislators and all executive and judicial officers of the national government and of the states, "shall be bound by Oath or Affirmation, to support this Constitution." But the truth is that few of them know much about what is in the Constitution. From time to time some will know a phrase or a clause from it that is topical in the public debate, a clause in isolation that becomes popular in the media. Almost none of them will have ever read or understood the Constitution itself. And few will care about the pledges they have made.

And yet, who elects these people of such vaporous integrity? The answer to "how did he get away with it?" is he got away with it because he could, and because the people let him.

What about recourse to the courts to overturn the theft? That was a waste of time. For all their lawyerly casuistry, they can be as indifferent to the Constitution as the others.

Several cases were brought to the courts by aggrieved parties who had been robbed in the gold grab. In one case the Supreme Court simply ruled against a plaintiff on the grounds that he would have had to resort to a gold market, but that such a gold market no longer existed. All the cases were decided on such hair-splitting grounds. It is furthermore no surprise that none of the cases the court elected to take up made a direct and central challenge to the constitutionality of the theft itself.

Now let us come back to why Roosevelt did it. It is often believed that the government's primary objective in the gold confiscation was to enrich itself: to pay $20.67 an ounce for gold that it would itself hoard at a new and much higher value. It is easy to understand this belief. Most of the gold confiscations throughout history had no other objective than robbery. At about the time of Roosevelt's theft, Stalin was torturing Russians to make them cough up their gold—for the sole purpose of enriching the Kremlin.

But for Roosevelt, it was something more grandiose. It was about something other than simply stealing the gold. He wanted to devalue the dollar and wanted to make the people dependent on the State. As both a reliable unit of value and as a safe haven against the general assault on the peoples' liberty, only gold stood in the way of a fiat currency. So, the objective was twofold: first, to devalue the dollar then and there, and then to get gold out of the way. Gold's role in the monetary system acted as a brake on the Fed expansion of money and credit and the endless growth of the State. It was an impediment to deficit spending and had to go. Gold had to go because it made the individual's financial well-being dependent upon himself, instead of upon State benefactors and the decrees of the monetary authorities. It was a bulwark against the erosion of property and individual rights. Gold had to go.

The New Dealers intended the devaluation of the dollar that resulted from raising the gold price to increase the price of other commodities, especially agricultural goods in an effort to secure farm votes. The devaluation achieved higher prices. But at the same time the New Deal's explosion of new bureaucracies and new regulations had the predictable effect of reduced production. And reduced production meant lower employment.

The Depression continued.

Despite the New Deal's brazen and sweeping attack on gold, no final victory against real money for free people could be declared. The dollar still had one last tie to gold. Roosevelt had made Americans who owned monetary gold into felons, but he had no such power over foreigners. They could still redeem their US dollars for gold. But this remaining tie to gold was not a powerful restraint on the Fed's money creation. It allowed the Fed to create enough unbacked money to reduce the purchasing power of the dollar by more than two-thirds before the last remaining link of the dollar to gold could finally be severed.

But severed by whom? Who was up to that tricky task? His 1968 campaign slogan had the answer:

"Nixon's the One!"

CHAPTER EIGHT
GOODBYE TO GOLD

What do you call someone who knowingly writes checks for money that is not in his account? Someone who stiffs the people he is pretending to pay? Intentionally writes checks that cannot be cashed, checks returned for insufficient funds?

What do you call such a person?

A cheat. A crook. Check-kiter. Liar. Thief. Con man. Paper-hanger. Swindler. There are a lot of terms for such a person. None are exactly flattering.

Now, what do you call a government that does the very same thing?

Honorable? Blameless? Typical? Corrupt? More than 150 years ago Frédéric Bastiat, the French economist and statesman, provided a pretty good rule of thumb for such things: see if the law allows the State to do what a citizen himself cannot do without committing a crime. If such practices are not abolished immediately, they "will spread, multiply, and develop into a system."

In some ways this part of the story of real money for free people is more damning than the shameless theft committed by the government under Roosevelt and his brain trust. In that case, the government stole the people's gold. But the people are the ones who selected the government that robbed them. Not only did the people elect Roosevelt by a landslide, but they also reelected him three more times. That is not much consolation for those who were not complicit in empowering the State or in electing Roosevelt; they were without blame and did not deserve to be victims.

But in the next episode, the story we tell in this chapter, the victims bore no responsibility for the crime syndicate that robbed them. That is because they were not Americans. They were people in other lands, robbed by a foreign government.

Ours.

THE CREATURES FROM BRETTON WOODS

This part of our story begins late in World War II, in July 1944, at a hotel in Bretton Woods, New Hampshire. The event was called the United Nations Monetary and Financial Conference. It has since been known at the Bretton Woods Conference. G. Edward Griffin called it a gathering of "the world's most prominent socialists." Just as a gathering in Georgia thirty-four years earlier gave birth to the Creature from Jekyll Island, the Federal Reserve, this gathering had several odious offspring.

The planners wanted a monstrous world government served by a single global bank as a means of bypassing national sovereignty (and necessarily individual sovereignty). So, the creatures they gave birth to at Bretton Woods included both the World Bank and the International Monetary Fund, as well as promulgating the Bretton Woods agreement. That accord created an international currency regime that sought to substitute the US dollar for gold.

The Bretton Woods collectivists, including John Maynard Keynes, spent weeks contriving to do to the world monetary system what the Federal Reserve had done in the United States. They sought to create a worldwide central bank that could issue global money out of nothing, just as the Fed does in the US.

For the record it should be noted that the lead architect of these Bretton Wood plans was a senior US Treasury official named Harry Dexter White. White was a member of the Communist Party and an active agent of the Soviets. He engaged in espionage against America, passing state secrets to Soviet intelligence. Despite overwhelming personal testimony and forensic evidence against White, his apologists in the media and others on the left protested his innocence for years.

But the evidence of his betrayal and communist sympathies just kept pouring out. More than fifty years after the Bretton Woods conference, the 1995 release of decoded Soviet spy network communications, the Venona intercepts, confirmed White's role as a Soviet agent, along with that of his counterpart in the State Department, the infamous Alger Hiss. Subsequent reviews of Kremlin archives accessed after the collapse of the Soviet Union confirmed the Venona intercepts.

It is self-evident that a global monetary scheme created by White, an agent of Soviet espionage since the mid-1930s, well before World War II, would hardly have been designed to advance the interests that free people have in sound money.

In brief, the monetary arrangement that resulted from this conclave of leftists was another centralized, authoritarian Rube Goldberg device. The British pound had been the respected world reserve currency until the Bank of England suddenly defaulted on the pound's redeemability in gold in September 1931. This reserve status meant that British pounds were used to settle accounts between nations, or as a reserve held by central banks against which they issued their own local currencies. The world reserve currency is a standard of international commerce, as well. For example, Persian Gulf oil producers accepted payment in pounds during the reign of the British currency. But since its founding OPEC, the petroleum cartel, has priced its production in dollars.

Britain's default was a betrayal of foreign nations, mostly European. Instead of relying on gold, they had trusted British monetary management and accepted its assurances. Just as they would again forty years later when they trusted the dollar, they suffered immense losses; the pound sterling quickly fell by 35 percent. David Stockman writes that once the pound defaulted its gold promises, "the world plunged into the dark night of economic nationalism, protectionism, fiat currencies, and economic stagnation."

We call that the Great Depression. The Bretton Woods response at the end of the war was to exploit American financial and military might and make the US dollar the new British pound, the new reserve currency of the world. Foreign nations would be able to hold their currency reserves in dollars this time, instead of in pounds or in gold. The Bretton Woods plan maintained that dollars would always be redeemable for gold at the rate of $35 an ounce. Or, stated differently, the dollar would be pegged to gold at that price, while other currencies would be pegged to the dollar. Something is always a substitute for something else in such schemes. Local currencies were substitutes for the dollar; the dollar was a substitute for gold. It should have been transparent that all this substitution was nothing more than a sleight of hand by the world monetary magicians. They could not manage gold, but they could regulate and manage the substitutes to their advantage and at the expense of the people. Their flimflam was evident from the beginning since Americans were already forbidden from exchanging their dollars for gold, and even prohibited from owning monetary gold at all. So, the guarantee of the dollar's perpetual redeemability was already built on a lie, one that disadvantaged firstly the American people.

But Bretton Woods went further. The dollar would be redeemable only by foreign governments and by their central banks. It was closed arrangement, a private club of governments, institutions famed for financial and monetary irresponsibility. Frozen out from redeemability were private businesses and individuals, those whose patterns of increased and lessened redemptions would signal how prudently the market judged the issuance of dollars. If the US issued paper dollars wantonly, out of proportion to the gold it claimed back those dollars, individual dollar holders should have been able to exchange their paper for gold. But under the Bretton Woods terms they could turn to the US Treasury and do—exactly nothing. While they were frozen out from exchanging promiscuously issued dollars for gold, they were nevertheless frozen into dependence on the currency schemes by legal tender laws and by the abrogation of private gold contracts.

Henry Hazlitt was a prominent *New York Times* editorial writer at the time. Quite unlike those who hold such positions today, he understood the linkage between sound money and national prosperity, was an admirer of Mises, and a man of eminent economic sensibility. He wrote that Bretton Woods was unworkable and would break down under the ensuing inflation that it enabled. For his troubles, he lost his job at the *Times*, a newspaper that has the distinction of being wrong about seemingly everything, from its cover-up of Stalin's starvation of Ukraine, to Fidel Castro, who it assured Americans was a mere agricultural reformer, to Saddam Hussein's non-existent WMDs. Wrong about all that and wrong about the Bretton Woods agreement, too.

Eventually the Bretton Woods standard began to unravel exactly as Hazlitt had predicted. By 1960 the market price of gold in London was $40.50 an ounce. How could that be if US dollars could be exchanged for gold for only $35 an ounce? But the official exchange rate was mostly an empty promise. By 1964 foreign governments had more dollars than the US could redeem for gold.

But the Federal Reserve was busy printing more money anyway, trying to accommodate the guns-and-butter deficit spending in Washington, characterized by President Johnson's Great Society and the Vietnam War.

In a denial of reality, eight central banks agreed to pool their gold, selling gold from the pool to depress the price of gold, to keep the market price close to $35. Of course, the American people's gold held by the Treasury provided half the gold to the London Gold Pool; seven European central banks provided the rest. But the demand for gold from foreign dollar holders was endless. On one day in March 1968, foreign holders took down $400 million of gold. It was thought to be a run on gold, but it was really dollar dumping. That the US was writing bad checks was an open secret, but the US long deluded itself in thinking that no one would challenge the global hegemony and enforce claims on the dollar. It was wrong. The Gold Pool had to be disbanded the next day.

IT'S ALWAYS ABOUT THE ELECTION

In 1971, President Nixon was leaning hard on the Fed to flood the economy with money to assure his reelection the next year. But as the printing presses rolled, dollar holders kept lining up to demand their gold claims. In August, the British ambassador showed up at the Treasury Department to convert $3 billion to gold. Of course, it was a futile effort and only days later, on August 15, President Nixon slammed the gold window shut, severing the last link of the dollar to gold.

It is worth noting that Roosevelt, a Democrat, began ditching gold. Nixon, a Republican, finished what Roosevelt had started. Where, one is forced to ask, is the American political party that wanted to preserve the dollar's purchasing power, standing for a dollar as good as gold? Of course, there isn't one, and as James Grant so wittily put it, "the dollar was now as good as paper."

Many believe that Nixon's act, which was technically an admission of US bankruptcy, was a product of his profound indifference; that Nixon didn't know what he was doing in delinking the dollar from gold, and that he didn't care, as long as the near-term result was to improve his prospects for reelection. Early in his first term, he instructed his chief of staff, H. R. Haldeman, that he did "not want to be bothered with international monetary matters... and will not need to see the reports on international money matters in the future."

To make clear that Nixon's remark was not just a one-off, but a symptom of his inattention, here is an Oval Office transcript from a few years later:

> **Haldeman:** Did you get the report that the British floated the pound last night?
>
> **President:** No. I don't think so.
>
> **Haldeman:** They did.
>
> **President:** That's devaluation?
>
> **Haldeman:** Yeah. Flannigan's got a report on it here.

President: I don't care about it. Nothing we can do about it.

Haldeman: You want a rundown?

President: No. I don't.

Haldeman: He argues it shows the wisdom of our refusal to consider convertibility until we get a new monetary system.

President: Good. I think he's right. It's too complicated for me to get into. God damn it (*unintelligible*) I understand.

Haldeman: Burns expects a five percent devaluation against the dollar.

President: Yeah. OK. Fine. Well...

Haldeman: Burns is concerned about speculation about the lira.

President: Well, I don't give a shit about the lira... (*unintelligible.*)

It would be charitable to call Nixon merely cavalier about the destructive forces he set in motion. A much more cynical interpretation is justified. One of the accounts from the August 15, 1971, debacle betrays Nixon's real priorities: his concern that his national address announcing the initiative would anger voters for preempting the popular Sunday night television western *Bonanza*. In their account of the episode in the book *Commanding Heights*, authors Daniel Yergin and Joseph Stanislaw write, "A few of the advisors would recollect that more time was spent discussing the timing of the speech than how the economic program would work."

Reflecting the worldwide impact of the policy change, it quickly became known as the Nixon Shock. In addition to refusing to cash the checks the US had written on its gold holdings, Nixon imposed a 10 percent surtax on all imports to the United States. He further imposed on Americans a regime of wage and price control. Although both the inflation and unemployment rates were high, around 6 percent, the surtax, like the devaluation of the dollar, raised prices for Americans on goods from overseas. At the same time, the price controls were imposed to keep a lid on prices.

In removing the dollar's gold backing, Nixon created economic chaos that not only unsettled the country at the time, but also resulted in repercussions which are only now ready to play out in a predictably destructive manner. His actions that summer left the civilized world for the first time in history without a single currency anchored to gold or silver; he paved the way for the highest peacetime inflation in American history; his unbacked dollar inexorably led to higher energy prices, with oil rising from $1.40 a barrel when Nixon took to the airwaves, to $13 per barrel four years later; and in attempting to suppress relentlessly climbing consumer prices he had himself enabled, he imposed a regime of wage and price controls and thereby created a shortage economy that rivaled wartime conditions.

Having let such genies out of the bottle, and faced with the stagflation conditions that resulted¬—a combination of high unemployment and high inflation—Arthur Burns, the Fed chairman in the Nixon years, remarked that "the old laws of economics aren't working like they used to." Of course, the economic laws were working fine. It was the Bretton Woods contraption and the Keynesian deficit spending doctrine that were flawed.

With the delinking of the dollar and gold, there was no discipline to serve as a brake on deficit spending. That part of the Bretton Woods agreement was gone. Forty years after the basic agreement broke down with the Nixon Shock, Hazlitt wrote that the Bretton Woods system "continues to do great harm because the dollar, though no longer based on gold and itself depreciating, continues to be used (as of this writing) as the world's primary reserve currency, while the institutions it set up, like the International Money Fund and the World Bank, continue to make immense new loans to irresponsible and improvident governments."

August 15, 1971 remains a watershed day in American economic history, one still noted for its folly. Ron Paul, the longtime congressman, presidential candidate, and leading champion of sound money and American liberty, was a young obstetrician at the time. "I remember the day very clearly," he said three decades later. It was the event that moved him, although reluctantly, to enter politics.

With gold completely absent from the monetary system, no longer able to protect the dollar against the State's devaluations, and no longer in place to slow the perpetual growth of deficits and debt, it was only a minor nuisance to the State. That is why there was not much resistance at the end of 1974, when President Gerald Ford issued an executive order repealing Roosevelt's order from forty years earlier commandeering the people's gold. To be sure, their gold was not restored to them or to their families, and it did not represent a return to gold in the US monetary system. But at least the private ownership of gold by Americans was legalized and Americans who owned monetary gold were no longer considered dangerous felons. However, the State was careful that the step did not allow gold to usurp its fiat money power. Ford's order specifically failed to allow the enforcement of contracts based on monetary gold.

After August 15, 1971, with the dollar officially a fiction that could be conjured up out of nothing, the 1970s proved to be a bull market blur for precious metals. It was completely foreseeable. With the Vietnam War and the Great Society, government growth, spending, and money-printing grew year after year and the price of everything climbed as a result. The price of gold was like a coiled spring.

In January 1973 gold peaked at $63.90 (the Dow Jones Industrial Average was 1051 that month).

As I described in the Preface, fresh out of high school I took my first, entry-level job in the gold business in 1973. The business was in its infancy then, and quite different. Since Roosevelt's 1934 gold confiscation had exempted numismatic coins and collections, American dealers had to concentrate on making a market in rare coins. In 1954, the United States Treasury ruled that all coins minted prior to 1933 were presumed to be rare, so it was those coins, foreign and domestic, that were the bulk of our business: US $10- and $20-dollar gold pieces (Eagles and Double Eagles), foreign mintings from before 1933, including British sovereigns, French and Swiss gold francs, and Mexican 50-peso gold coins.

Although the one-ounce gold South African Krugerrand introduced in 1967 was clearly a bullion coin, it was also a legal tender coin in South Africa, so it began to find its way into the hands of American investors. Soon it would be the most widely owned gold coin in the world. The company I was a principal of quickly established a big footprint in the industry, and later became a primary dealer for the South African Chamber of Mines and was selected to introduce its new products.

When gold ownership was finally legalized, after the last day of 1974, the gold price surged to $195, looking suspiciously like the money center institutions had driven the price up so that Americans, eager to own gold after more than forty years of arbitrary and unconstitutional prohibitions, would have to buy it at the top of the market. Twenty-one months later, in September 1976, it had fallen to $103.

After that, the price never looked back for the rest of the decade. By January 1980, less than three and a half years later, gold had tipped the scale at $850. Along the way other countries minted one-ounce bullion coins that began to follow the Krugerrand into the hands of gold-starved Americans: the Canadian Gold Maple Leaf in 1979, the Chinese Gold Panda in 1982, and the American Gold Eagle in 1986, now the most popular of gold coins.

But victory over real money for free people could not be declared with the elimination of gold alone from the US monetary system. As you will recall from Chapter Three, "The Free Republic is Born," the framers correctly insisted that silver be included in the Constitution's reference to coinage.

How could the Federal Reserve and its fiat money scheme hope to prevail if silver had been allowed to remain in the picture? In the next chapter, we will loop back around to show you how silver had already been carefully removed from America's currency. And I will reveal a little about a plan to corner the world's silver market.

It is a story I know well.

Firsthand.

CHAPTER NINE
SO LONG, SILVER!

When George Washington signed the Coinage Act of 1792, the US dollar was established as the official currency of the United State. It was defined as a silver coin of 371 ¼ grains of pure silver, or just over .77 troy ounces. In other words, it adopted the value and quality of the Spanish silver dollar, which was one of the most reliable coins and the de facto currency of the America people at that time. You might remember that Spanish silver dollars were prized and referred to as "pieces of eight" in the pirate movies.

With that, real money for free people was off to a good start. Details of silver's subsequent history in the US monetary system are beyond the scope of this book except to mention that it was often a convoluted mess of crony capitalism as the government continually interfered with silver prices and with its supply and demand, which yielded predictable consequences of distortions, both shortages and mountains of surpluses.

But of the original US dollar we must mention two things that illustrate an admirable depth of early Americans' understanding of the centrality of sound money to their freedom. The original US coins bore the inscription "Liberty," and an allegorical image of the spirit of Liberty. The coinage act also imposed a death penalty for debasing US gold or silver coins.

The evolution of today's silver coin and bullion market followed a different path from that of gold. In the early 1960s the government set the price of silver at $1.29, determined to sell silver if it rose above that price, and thereby drive the price back down. It was a fool's errand. In a few short years it was forced to dump 1.6 billion ounces in a futile attempt to keep the price down. Finally, in 1967 the government threw in the towel. The price of silver kept rising.

The rising price was, of course, a consequence of relentless money-printing and dollar debauchery. By the mid-1960s the US dollar was worth only 31 percent of the value it had when the Federal Reserve was created in 1913, so its rising price was entirely foreseeable when President Johnson issued an executive order in 1964 to end silver's role in the US monetary system. Except for some half-dollars minted with sharply reduced silver content until 1970, silver coinage in US currency ended in 1965. In its stead, the government began minting base metal coins with no silver content, although the mint went to great lengths to create the appearance of silver in the new coinage.

THE ROAD TO FUNNY MONEY

Johnson had done to US monetary silver what Roosevelt and Nixon had done to gold. When Johnson signed the US Coinage Act in a Rose Garden ceremony in 1965 ratifying his executive order, he insisted that the real silver coins would trade side-by-side with the new base metal coins forever.

> If anybody has any idea of hoarding our silver coins, let me say this. Treasury has a lot of silver on hand, and it can be, and it will be used to keep the price of silver in line with its value in our present silver coin. There will be no profit in holding them out of circulation for the value of their silver content.

If the president believed what he said, he was deluded. If he did not believe it, he was a liar. There was indeed great profit to be had in holding the real silver coins, and they began to disappear from circulation at once. The people began habitually going through the change that passed their way, holding on to the real silver and spending and passing along the cheap coins. As inflation drove the price of silver (and everything else) higher, real silver coins became a popular investment vehicle, a preferred way to hold silver. The pre-1965 dimes, quarters, and half-dollars began to be traded in "bags" with a face value of $1,000, meaning either 10,000 dimes, 4,000 quarters, or 2,000 half dollars. These bags, weighing about 55 pounds, each contained about 715 ounces of actual silver content. Since they were circulated coins, not collector coins, the bags became known in the trade as "junk silver" or "junk bags."

Remember that anyone could have gathered those coins at their face value from daily circulation in 1964, a bag of which would have amounted to $1,000. By the time I left my first job in the precious metals brokerage industry and become a principal in a new company in the summer 1974, the price of silver had settled in at about $4 an ounce. A bag of silver was worth close to $2,900. Johnson's assurance that there was no profit in holding on to the real silver coins was typical Washington balderdash.

Between ending the dollar's ties to gold and removing silver from the monetary system, too, a justifiable distrust in governmental monetary management began to grow. Rising inflation and stagnant economic conditions gave rise to one of the most dramatic episodes in precious metals history. And I had a front row seat.

Actually, it was more than a front row seat. I was a participant. I had a seat at the table.

THE HUNT BROTHERS

The billionaire Hunt brothers, Nelson Bunker Hunt (who was often called a real-life J. R. Ewing), William Herbert Hunt, and Lamar Hunt, sons of the fabled oilman H. L. Hunt, began to have concerns about the long-term viability of the dollar. They had taken sizeable positions in silver in 1974. But by 1979 their concerns about the dollar were growing, concerns that were justified by events and even shared by the Bank of International Settlement, the central bankers' central bank, which had begun wagging its finger at US practices.

In an explicit attempt to hedge against dollar mischief, in 1979 the Hunt brothers, along with a couple of Arab oil sheiks and other international players, began determinedly buying silver.

They bought a lot of silver.

This caught the attention of the Federal Reserve. The Fed quietly informed the commodity exchanges that they took a dim view of this activity on the grounds that it was weakening the dollar in international markets. This was typical Fed hogwash. It was the Fed's own handiwork, the destruction of the value of the dollar, that was driving the Hunts and others to protect themselves with silver. That view was corroborated by Saudis close to royal family who began buying silver as well. They had been selling oil, their valuable natural resource, for a currency of crumbling value; some had decided to protect their proceeds with silver, another natural resource but one with monetary virtues.

At the beginning of 1979, the price of silver was a few cents over $6 an ounce. By the end of 1979 Bunker and Herbert Hunt and their companies had a silver position of more than 192 million ounces; they maintained that their average cost was only $10 an ounce. Every dollar increase in the silver price meant more than $190 million dollars for the brothers. By the middle of January 1980, silver reached $50 an ounce.

If we include the Saudis and a few other major overseas players who were buying silver at the same time and in much the same manner as the Hunt brothers, these interests controlled 280 million ounces. Writer Stephen Fay imagined what this much silver would have been like if it had all been bullion bars gathered together:

> Two hundred and eighty thousand 1,000-ounce bars of bullion, measuring 12 ½ x 5 ½ x 3 ½ inches would, piled on top of each other, have risen into the stratosphere 81,777 feet, almost double the cruising altitude of the *Concorde*. Laid end to end, the bars

would have stretched about 55 miles, roughly the distance from London to Oxford, or Boston to Providence.

But of course the Hunt's silver was not in one place. They bought silver in Switzerland. They bought silver in London. The bought silver in Chicago and New York. And it was not all in the form of bullion bars. The bought silver bars, silver forward contracts, silver futures contracts, and silver options.

And they bought silver coins. Which is where I came in.

An important part of Bunker's strategy was to acquire US silver coins, the "bags" described earlier. His strategy was shrewd and sound. Those silver bags were selling for negative premiums, which is for less than the melt value of their silver. He liked buying silver below the silver price. When the opportunity to take on Bunker Hunt's acquisition of silver bags arose, we were already in a powerful bull market in both silver and gold, and we had thousands of clients that needed all of our efforts to get them the lowest prices in the market when they wanted to buy, and the highest possible prices available when they needed to sell. But the opportunity to be a part of the Hunt's silver buying was impossible to resist.

The scope of the Hunt project is hard to convey. Silver futures traded on the Comex market in contracts of 5,000 ounces. So, if the Hunts bought 100 contracts—and they had thousands of such contracts—their silver holding grew by 500,000 ounces in just one transaction executed at one place, at one time.

Silver bags were a quite different story. They had to be purchased from dealers and investors and collectors across the country and around the world, often one bag of about 715 ounces of silver at a time. So, in addition to the daily demands of a record-setting bull market, my trading staff and I in Phoenix devoted enormous efforts between October 1979 and January 1980 to buying bags of silver coins for the most audacious silver accumulating enterprise in history. Day and night, early and late, we were on the phone around the world locking in order after order for Bunker Hunt and having the silver shipped to Phoenix.

One of our brokers told me that while he understood intellectually how much silver we were acquiring for Hunt, it was only a number to him until he visited the vaults one night and saw with his own eyes the mountains of silver our security crews were receiving, moving, stacking, and storing. He was left speechless.

We bought 7,000 bags of 90 percent US silver coins (dimes, quarters, and half-dollars), 4,000 bags of US silver dollars, and 3,000 bags of 40 percent silver Kennedy half-dollars.

Altogether in late 1979 and early 1980 we bought $250 million worth of silver coins for Bunker Hunt. That would be the equivalent of about $900 million in today's dollars.

Gold and silver are sensitive barometers of world-changing events and I have experienced many in my years in the business, including the market chaos and volatility when fifty-two Americans were taken hostage in Iran and the spiking markets when President Reagan was shot. In the weeks right after Donald Trump was elected, gold fell more than $150 an ounce, on the view that the debt and money printing would be brought under control. That has not happened, and gold has been higher ever since. But nothing compares to being a part of the biggest event that had ever occurred in the history of the commodity markets when the Hunt brothers tried to corner the world silver market.

There is a crucial lesson to be learned from the rest of the Hunt brothers' silver story. The commodity exchanges and regulators took unprecedented steps to strip the Hunts of their silver, among them instituting a sudden "liquidation only rule." That meant that the exchanges would only allow silver to be sold. It meant that those with "long" positions—net holders of silver like the Hunts—were forced to sell to the "shorts," those who had sold silver they did not own at lower prices, silver they could not deliver.

How can an exchange that exists for buyers and sellers to come together function fairly when only liquidation is allowed? For those interested, the definitive account of the entire affair can be found in the book *Silver Bulls: The Great Silver Boom and Bust* by Paul Sarnoff. Sarnoff writes that the Hunts and other silver buyers had no one to sell to except those who had made the brazen and self-serving sell-only rule:

The longs now had no place to go, no normal market to absorb their holdings. They found themselves now locked in perilously by Comex rules—rules formulated by the board including at least four members representing firms that held the majority portion of the shorts....

It was a devious move by those on the wrong side of the market, a thinly disguised form of robbery and one taken in conjunction with the government authorities. For example, the Federal Reserve effectively "redlined" gold and silver credit sources, a move that further disabled the Hunts.

COUNTERPARTY RISK

I have described these events in some detail, not only because they were important experiences in my own career but because of what they teach about real money for free people.

Gold and silver are the only monetary assets that are not someone else's liability. They are not dependent on someone else's solvency, promises to perform, or honesty. Their value does not depend on the endorsement, propriety, or honesty of any State or institution. They have no counterparty risk, no risk of rule changes, nonpayment, default, or bankruptcy by individuals, companies, financial exchanges, institutions, and banks—quite apart from being insulated from the risks of the Fed's fiat dollar as well.

It is a wonderful thing for people's promises to be reliable, for institutions to be vigorous fiduciaries of their clients' interest. The modern world with all its miracles is built on the assurance that people will meet their obligations, fulfill their contracts, and respect others' property.

When this environment of trust begins to fray, sophisticated civilization itself is at risk.

The Hunt incident is a naked example of the sort of counterparty risk that can pop up anywhere and at any time. Proliferating counterparty risks lead wise investors to the safe haven of gold and silver. But their unique advantage only applies to physical precious metals, the gold and silver coins and bullion that you own outright and have taken into your own possession. It does not extend to paper gold, stocks, and other representations of gold ownership, commodity contracts, ETFs, or precious metals controlled by a fund, bank, or exchange. Or any other investment vehicle in which State cronies can change the rules in the middle of the game.

In a congressional hearing after the affair that stripped the Hunts of their silver, Bunker Hunt was asked by a senator what it was like to lose a billion dollars.

"A billion dollars ain't what it used to be, Senator," he replied.

Bunker Hunt died in 2014 at the age of 88.

With this chapter we have completed our account of the framers' wise constitutional provision of real money for free people, its contribution to American prosperity, and how it has been undone, both with the elimination of gold from our monetary system at the hands of Franklin Roosevelt and Richard Nixon, along with the abandonment of silver.

The US dollar has remained unmoored, unanchored, untied to anything real ever since. Unlike fiat currencies that have gone before, the dollar is the ultimate fiat currency. It is global in scope because it is world's reserve currency. At the same time, the United States is the biggest debtor in history.

It remains only to describe where we are today and how it all ends.

CHAPTER TEN
THE ENDGAME

Our story of real money for free people has come full circle now. We started with tales of monetary madmen from other places and other times, described their corruption of money, and noted that even the US has its own "print first, think later" madmen.

We told of gold's superiority to paper money and something of its role in the monetary systems of the most free and accomplished civilizations. Next, we focused on the intentions of the American founders in creating for us a monetary system composed of gold and silver.

Along the way we paused to acknowledge the unique qualities of gold and silver. We enjoyed describing gold and silver not in the material reductionist manner so typical of our age, but holistically, providing a more complete picture that helps explain why nothing else fills a monetary role as perfectly as precious metals.

Then it was on to provide you with an account of the creation of the central bank, the Federal Reserve, as the crony banksters sought a money monopoly for themselves. Like mob bosses unleashing gangland warfare to secure their crime monopolies, the State moved ruthlessly, plundering and stealing over the decades to eliminate the competition of sound money and the discipline it enforces on financial affairs.

By now you should have realized that central banks and fiat money are managed for the greater glory of the State and for the special advantage of the State's cronies, and not for the benefit of the people. Inflation is the means by which the State enriches itself by subterfuge, quietly eroding the purchasing power of the currency for its own benefit. And while inflation itself is actually the State's increase of the supply of money and credit, it is the effects of that increase—higher prices because of the currency's failing purchasing power—that people call inflation.

The destruction of a currency's purchasing power is evidence of the currency system's failure.

We are at the end of our tale, except to describe where we are today. And I am afraid the news is not good. We do not have real money, a monetary system that could have served as a bulwark against the usurpations of the State. And after several generations of being under assault by the State on every front, it is safe to say that the light of liberty has dimmed, that the fires of freedom do not appear to burn brightly in the hearts of many of the American people.

And so, the monetary system of fraudulent, legalized counterfeiting has now been allowed to reach its logical extreme and will now collapse of its unrestrained excesses and deceit.

To some it may appear melodramatic to announce that we are at a monetary endgame. But it is clear-eyed realism that follows from the historical precedents. And from the hard accounting.

So far in this book we have relied on telling the story of real money for free people entirely as a narrative. But since this story needs to be told holistically too, we will finish with a few numbers to help make our trajectory clear and our account complete.

THE DEBT BUBBLE

The federal government owes about $34 trillion. This is quite an achievement. After all, those trillions had to be borrowed. And borrowed they were, even though every lender knows that none of it can ever be paid back except by borrowing more money tomorrow to pay off the portion of the bill that comes due today.

It is a Ponzi scheme, and one that is astonishing to have persisted as long as it has.

Think about how fast the spending has ramped up in our time. America won its independence in the Revolutionary War, fought the War of 1812, completed the Louisiana Purchase, bought Alaska, and fought a Civil War; it opened the west and expanded to the Pacific coast; it fought the Spanish-American War, won two world wars, fought wars in Korea and Vietnam, and put a man on the moon—all without accumulating a national debt of $1 trillion.

The entire federal debt did not reach $1 trillion until 1982—and I do not mean the one-year spending deficit. I mean that the *entire* accumulated debt of the federal government did not reach $1 trillion until 1982. That was in President Reagan's first term. Then the debt broke above $10 trillion at the end of Bush the Younger's presidency. It rose to $20 trillion at the end of Obama's tenure.

Think about just the last part: the federal debt doubled during the Obama presidency.

Since then, the national debt grew by about a trillion dollars a year until 2020. Then, with the Covid-19 shutdown, it grew by more than $3.2 trillion during the 2020 fiscal year alone.

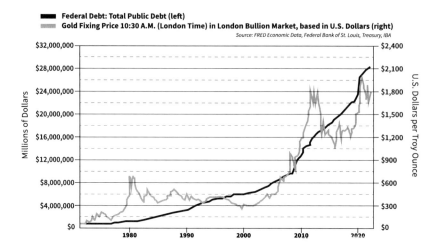

Federal Debt: Total Public Debt (left)
Gold Fixing Price 10:30 A.M. (London Time) in London Bullion Market, based in U.S. Dollars (right)

Source: FRED Economic Data, Federal Bank of St. Louis, Treasury, IBA

To describe the sudden explosion in federal debt in less than a decade, consider this.

At a recent gold price of $2,000, all the gold that has ever been mined in history—all the gold from ancient Lydia, mined in Egypt of the pharaohs, all the gold stolen by the conquistadors in the new world, all the gold from the gold rush—in short all the gold ever found in all of recorded history, and in all the continents of the world, all the world's gold could be purchased with just the amount of debt that the United States has accumulated in the last five years.

Throughout its history, US debt has averaged 30 percent of total US economic output. Today, it is over 120 percent, more than four times the average. It is more than the entire annual productivity of China, Japan, Germany, the United Kingdom, France, and Italy combined.

Or to put it in yet another way, the US national debt is equal to $102,400 per citizen, or $409,000 for a family of four. That is a substantial mountain of debt to try to service, considering that the median US income (half the people are below it, half above) is only $40,000.

The US debt situation is hopeless. In fact, it is worse than $34 trillion. In addition to the acknowledged debt, the government has made all kinds of other promises to pay for things like Social Security and Medicare. This hidden debt, the unfunded liabilities of the government, runs somewhere between five and ten times the visible debt.

This is an existential issue for this country, one so advanced and alarming that Washington politicians' hair should all be on fire! Instead, they are mostly quiet as tiny mice. There is little or no coalition in Congress to control the raging debt growth, which is further evidence that *no one any longer believes that anything can be done to bring things under control*, short of engaging in a massive monetary fraud.

That is the only way out for the authorities. And they know it. They will have to try to inflate the debt away. That means they will print more and more dollars to pay the debt, catastrophically reducing the value of the dollar, shredding the fabric of social life and commercial trust, and impoverishing the American people along the way.

For the State it has now come to this: inflate or die!

That means that if the State does not inflate, it will effectively repudiate its debt, and the State itself, at least in its present form, will cease to exist and usher in a revolution along the way.

Debt repudiation or an overt default is not an option any bureaucrat or central banker willingly chooses. It is too sudden. It disempowers them at once. Inflating the currency to worthlessness stalls the decay and creates in them the illusion that they remain in charge of events, especially if the public can be made to believe that the currency destruction has an exogenous or external cause (while the responsible authorities themselves escape like thieves in the night).

This is the situation that Gideon Gono was in in Zimbabwe. It is the same situation that Rudolf von Havenstein faced in Germany a century ago.

It is Jerome Powell's situation today. It is inflate or die.

Those are some of the reasons why foreigners' faith in the dollar is in decline. That is why there is a global movement away from the dollar.

That is why foreign central banks and governments, and individuals around the world, buy gold with money they used to keep in US dollars. Today's movement out of the dollar is just a trickle. It will soon be a flood. Few people notice the trickle. They will awaken one day to the flood and wonder what happened. But if you pay attention, you will be able to watch as today's trickle grows and the flood waters approach.

THE MADE-UP MONEY BUBBLE

The numbers printed on the face of currencies elsewhere may have had more zeros appended to them, but in terms of the real wealth being debauched and subverted, we are in a money and credit bubble of historic proportions. We are living witnesses to the most massive eruption of unbacked, digital printing press money the world has ever seen. It has been pumped into the economy so recklessly as to defy belief.

The Federal Reserve has been engaged in pure Gonoism. Just like Gono, it is printing trillions of dollars. But it is not the currency of a little banana republic that is involved. It is the reserve currency of the world.

Worse yet, it cannot stop printing money. The genie cannot be put back in the bottle.

On the following page is a chart of Federal Reserve assets. You notice that the graph turned straight up in 2020 and continues to climb today. It represents the things the Fed owns, more than $8.8 trillion worth of financial instruments of one kind or another: government bonds, mortgage securities, and other debt instruments, including junk bonds.

The Fed acquired all these things by purchasing them.

"Hey, wait a minute!" you might say. "Where did the Fed get all the money to buy all those things?"

Good question.

It printed the money. Well, it printed it digitally. But still it just made it up.

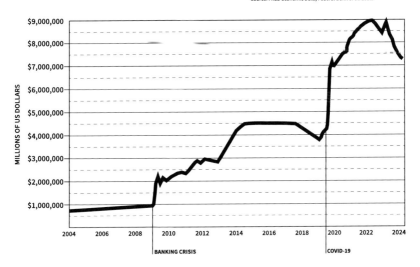

Total Assets (Less Eliminations from Consolidation): Wednesday Level (WALCL)

Source: FRED Economic Data, Federal Bank of St. Louis

Beginning on the left-hand side of the chart, you can see Fed assets had been very stable for a very long time at less than a trillion dollars. Suddenly, with the mortgage meltdown you can see Fed assets quickly jumped more than a trillion dollars. The Federal Reserve reacted to the mortgage meltdown in 2008 by creating $4 trillion in a program called quantitative easing (QE). It was all just made-up digital money. It did this so that it could buy toxic mortgages and other bonds from the crony banks. As we described in Chapter Six, one of the founding objectives of the Fed was to have the taxpayers cover the banking cartels' inevitable losses. And boy oh boy, did it ever help the crony banks out with QE!

The spree lasted from 2008 to 2014.

Recognizing the inflationary potential of that liquidity when it starts finding its way into the commercial banks and into the consumer economy, the Fed decided to try to undo what it had done before a nightmare inflation set in.

But it did not take long for the Fed to discover it had painted itself into a corner.

When the Fed tried to roll back some of its money printing in 2018 (you can see the line of the graph begins to trend slightly lower), the stock market threw a fit. Since stocks had been climbing for years on the back of free money for Wall Street, as the Fed tightened and reduced its assets, the market began to collapse. The S&P500 had traded as high as 2,941 points in late September 2018; by Christmas Eve it was 2,350, *a staggering 20 percent loss in only three months!*

Wall Street was on strike! More free money, it told the Fed, or we will bring the whole stock market house of cards down.

The Fed got the message. As you can see on the chart, the Fed's balance sheet began to notably grow once again in 2019. The Fed knows it must print money or the stock market will go into free fall. The Fed has become the guarantor of stock market profits. The Fed has become Wall Street's towel boy.

Eventually a critical mass of investors will figure this out. Discovering that the market is only held aloft by the Fed, they will head for the door all at once. And there is nothing the Fed can do at that point.

But in the meantime, in 2020 along came COVID-19.

The Fed stomped on the money-printing accelerator!

As you can see on the right side of the chart, Fed assets went completely "hockey stick," turning straight up. In no time at all, the Fed created more than $4.5 trillion with nothing more than a few digital keystrokes.

The Federal Reserve has taken this country's economy into extremely dangerous territory. It is not enough for us to say that we do not believe the Federal Reserve has any idea what it has done with these policies. It is better that you should know that the Fed itself *admits* it does not know what it has done. Efforts to roll back all of that money printing have been inadequate with Fed assets still almost $7.7 tillion.

We will simply quote Fed chairman Jerome Powell as the 2020 hockey stick operation was underway:

"We're not even thinking about thinking about the consequences of our actions."

Gideon Gono never made quite so brazen an admission.

THE GOVERNING CLASSES

Today spending is the sole political virtue among both Republicans and Democrats. Washington spends two dollars for every dollar it collects in taxes. The Fed backstops this recklessness, manipulating interest rates down to accommodate massive government borrowing, and printing money where it must to fill the gap created by the State's deficit spending. This is what the Fed calls "using the full range of its tools."

Both Fed money-printing and federal debt are evidence of severe character deficiencies among the American governing classes.

Fed money printing is a slap in the face of normal, healthy human interactions. Civilization is built on the implicit understanding that one may achieve his own ends by serving others. The butcher does not eat all that meat himself. The baker does not need all that bread. The candlestick maker has no use for all those candles himself. The things people in all their diversity want in satisfaction of their personal objectives are most readily achieved by the earnings they derive from providing goods and services others want, giving fair value for value received. But the proponents and beneficiaries of money printing are involved in a brazen attempt to take something for nothing, to acquire purchasing power by monetary manipulation, for which they provide nothing in return.

It is much the same with government debt. It allows for present consumption, while shuffling the bill off to future generations. Normal, healthy people try to leave something to their children and grandchildren. The framers of the Constitution wrote that their aim was to "secure the Blessings of Liberty to ourselves and our Posterity," for those to come. But a perverse generation burdens little children who have no say-so in the matter with debt that they must bear all their lives at the expense of their own prosperity.

The founders created the conditions for an explosion of human prosperity. Our governing classes and monetary authorities are their opposites. They have created the conditions for an explosion of impoverishment. They are the big spenders and reckless borrowers of both parties. They are the grand councilors and academic advisors of the almighty State. They and their statist epigone and media servitors are the inevitable offspring of connivers like Franklin Roosevelt and Richard Nixon, who stole the people's gold and betrayed the nation's good-as-gold dollar. They are a generation of trousered apes who do not know the difference between ditchwater and champagne, and of like-minded Fed officials who conflate empty paper promises with the real, enduring monetary wealth of the ages, who trade the real money of free people for a mess of monetary pottage.

By their own logic, there is no turning back. They must now continue to print money until the system crashes. It is the endgame of their folly.

They are the American Gonos. Gold and silver are your only protection from their imbecility and ruination.

APPENDIX I
GOLD VS. SILVER

It is generally believed, following the Greek historian Herodotus, that the first precious metal coins were from Lydia, rough lumps made of electrum, an alloy of both gold and silver together, and often stamped with animal images such as a lion's head.

Not long thereafter, Lydia's King Croesus, who is remembered in the literary expression still heard today, "rich as Croesus," refined the concept of coinage by minting coins of standardized purity of gold and of silver separately.

Having coins of both gold and silver in circulation created a challenge: how to compare the value of one coin with another. (When the ratio is set by law, rather than the market, it is a problem that has lasted through the ages, and one that caused a political uproar in America 125 years ago.) The coins of Croesus, and the later Persian coins under Darius the Great were decreed to have a fixed-weight exchange rate of about 13 silver to one gold.

But exchange rates are a product of place and time. Early Egyptians seem not to even have had a word for silver. Later, and apparently more rare to them at the time, silver seems to have been more valuable than gold. During Egypt's Middle Kingdom, around 3,600 years ago, silver's value was about half that of gold.

When Sir Isaac Newton was Britain's Master of the Royal Mint, he attempted to fix the ratio at 15.5 to one.

The United States Constitution, as we have seen, established gold and silver as legal tender in 1787, but wisely did not attempt to fix their exchange ratio. But as other countries had done, and at Treasury Secretary Alexander Hamilton's urging, Congress fixed the gold-silver exchange rate in 1792 at 15 to one; it was later changed to 16 to one.

After the Civil War and the greenback dollar debacle, the US returned to a simple gold standard. But by the end of the 1800s, there was a move driven by forces in silver-producing states to remonetize silver. Silver producers had no trouble selling their production at market prices, but they wanted the government to intervene, remonetizing silver at higher prices, boosting demand, and providing them a windfall. It would be an inflationary move, designed to substantially increase the money supply with the addition of unlimited silver coinage as legal tender. Farmers thought the increase in the currency would increase agricultural prices; debtors hoped it would devalue their debts.

But as the present era of money printing will demonstrate once again, inflationary policies do not always deliver what their adherents hope for, as Mises explained in *The Theory of Money and Credit*:

> What people are really asking for is a rise in the prices of those commodities and services they are selling while the prices of those commodities and services which they are buying remain unchanged. The potato grower aims at higher prices for potatoes. He does not long for a rise in other prices. He is injured if these other prices rise sooner or in greater proportion than the price of potatoes. If a politician addressing a meeting declares that the government should adopt a policy which makes prices rise, his

hearers are likely to applaud. Yet each of them is thinking of a different price rise.

From time immemorial inflation has been recommended to alleviate the burdens of poor worthy debtors at the expense of rich harsh creditors. However, under capitalism the typical debtors are not the poor but the well-to-do owners of real estate, of firms, and of common stock, people who have borrowed from banks, savings banks, insurance companies, and bondholders. The typical creditors are not the rich but people of modest means who own bonds and savings accounts or have taken out insurance policies. If the common man supports anti-creditor measures, he does it because he ignores the fact that he himself is a creditor.

The inflationist Free Silver Movement became the social justice cause of its day and was the central issue at the Democratic Party convention in 1896. It was there that William Jennings Bryan, a skilled orator who had been speaking for the Free Silver Movement across the country, gave his famous "Cross of Gold" speech. He electrified the convention, likening the gold standard to a crown of thorns on the brow of labor, and a cross upon which mankind was being crucified.

Bryan unexpectedly won the presidential nomination on the fifth ballot. He was defeated in the general election by William McKinley. Eventually the Gold Standard Act made gold the currency standard.

Attempting to establish a fixed equivalency between the two metals as Alexander Hamilton had done was, like all government price fixing, a mistake. Silver's monetary virtues, as we have discussed, are great. But the laws of supply and demand are great as well. They insist that prices be free to fluctuate and thereby convey real and vital information about supply and demand.

In a free market, the value of each metal is a function of its own separate fundamentals, according to which the exchange rate will vary. An event like the California gold rush would increase the supply of gold, while the popularity of photography later spiked the demand for silver.

Fixed exchange bimetallism will overvalue one metal at one time, undervaluing it at another. If the precious metal of one coinage climbs above the government rate, it will be hoarded or melted down and sold at the commodity price. The cheaper metal will be spent, used to pay creditors. It is an example of Gresham's Law, that bad money drives out good; when there are competing currencies, or currencies fixed at artificial rates, people will prize the superior currency, hold on to it, and pass along the inferior currency with their spending. Artificial prices and ratios cannot accommodate the realities of a dynamic economy.

Left to move freely, the gold-silver ratio has moved from one-to-one in ancient times to as high as 131 ounces of silver to one ounce of gold in 2020.

The ratio between the two metals is obtained simply by dividing the gold price by the silver price, resulting in how many ounces of silver it takes to buy one ounce of gold at a given time. This is a valuable tool for investors who wish to emphasize their holdings of the precious metal poised for the fastest appreciation.

The gold-silver ratio does not tell you where the price of either metal will be next month or next year, or indeed if prices will be higher or lower. But it can be a good guide to managing gold and silver investments. For example, when silver is underpriced relative to the gold price based on historical and recent movements in their relative prices, it is a favorable time to trade gold for silver.

To illustrate the strategy, suppose when the ratio is 80 to one you had 10 ounces of gold and you agreed to trade it for 800 ounces of silver. Then, sometime down the road as prices change, imagine that the ratio moved to 50 to one. At that time, you could trade that 800 ounces of silver back into 16 ounces of gold, instead of the ten ounces you started with. In this hypothetical exchange, you would have increased the amount of gold you own by sixty percent.

This example, using the spot prices of gold and silver, is for purposes of illustration only, given transaction costs and the fact that different coins and bars have their own premiums relative to the spot prices. But it demonstrates a strategy many of our clients, precious metals professionals, and I, myself, have used to substantially increase our precious metals holdings.

Modern experience indicates that in periods of inflation, silver moves quickly back into a monetary role. This was the case in the monetary destruction of the stagflation decade, the 1970s. Silver demand surged as a defense against the authorities' wanton dollar destruction. Both gold and silver moved higher, but silver moved faster, and the ratio moved lower, dipping below 15:1 in early 1980. Later, as the Volcker Federal Reserve tried to wring inflation out of the dollar, the ratio moved above 100:1 in 1981.

In the wake of the money-printing madness following the housing meltdown and the Great Recession, the gold-silver ratio dropped to 31:1 in 2011. Later, in early 2020, the ratio had moved up to a historically unprecedented 131:1. But with the money printing and deficit financed federal spending of 2020 that exploded in March, the ratio began to fall once again to much lower levels.

In the unlikely event that some amazing psychic had managed to somehow catch both the very low and the very high ratios of this nine-year cycle, a hypothetical trade at 31:1 would have seen him exchange 3,100 ounces of silver for 100 ounces of gold. Later, with the ratio at 131:1, he would have traded his gold back into 13,100 ounces of silver, more than quadrupling his silver holdings.

In addition to describing this gold-silver ratio history as a means of sharing with you a simple precious metals strategy that can be profitable, it illustrates a couple of other things.

While the prices of silver and gold are closely correlated, silver is more volatile than gold. True to its quicksilver nature, it moves fast. Silver often slumbers, its monetary qualities overlooked and its price lagging. But at some point, in a crisis, it awakens. Thanks to its liquidity and the other qualities we have described, people turn to silver, and it steps easily back into its time-honored role as a monetary asset. During those periods you can emphasize silver in your portfolio with confidence.

In a complete breakdown, silver can readily serve as a convenient currency as well. At $2,000 an ounce, a one-tenth ounce gold coin, about the smallest practical size gold coin, is worth about $200. If that is not suitable for everyday purchases, silver easily fills the needed function of smaller units of purchasing power.

This is something that those who are belittled as "survivalists" understand. (What exactly deserves shaming about making plans to survive dislocations in daily life is beyond us. Were many of us not taught as Boy Scouts to "be prepared"? Apparently, the lesson we learned of the grasshopper and the ants has been forgotten. But in an age of irresponsible grasshoppers, being industrious and prepared, like the ants in the story, is thought foolish.)

Those who do foresee unexpected and unwelcome currency upsets have long favored the US silver coins, dimes, quarters, and half dollars with a 90 percent silver content that were minted before 1965. Those coins are not collectibles or numismatic coins. They are circulated coins, some even well-worn, that were used as everyday currency until 1965. As we have described, they trade at prices based on their silver content. Since they are instantly recognizable, they do not need to be assayed, and unlike larger silver bars, the represent small units of purchasing power.

The survivalists may be proven right. If so, it will hardly be the first time in history. In any case, there is room in a well-balanced portfolio for both gold and silver, in proportions that can be modified to meet prevailing conditions.

APPENDIX II
REPUBLIC MONETARY EXCHANGE

I hope you have found this book to be informative and that it will be profitable for you as well. As I wrote in the Preface, it is my wish that it will "pay forward" some of the blessings and opportunities that life has provided me along the way.

I founded Republic Monetary Exchange to be a firm unlike others, to provide superior precious metals brokerage services to gold and silver buyers and sellers, to help them secure their futures, and to provide generational wealth protection. And because we have been in the business a very long time, we have a practiced eye for the financial and geopolitical developments that move the markets, knowledge born of experience that we are pleased to put to work for our friends and clients. If we can provide personal service second to none, and the most advantageous prices to our clients, both when they buy and when they sell, we feel we have done our job well.

Over the years thousands of people have bought and sold gold and silver from Republic Monetary Exchange. We offer each client a personal Account Executive to provide them with private and confidential service and ongoing consultation about their investment needs and overall long-term goals. We prioritize engaging our clients with seminars, online briefings, and market updates.

Republic Monetary Exchange subscribes to "best practices" for clients. That means our clients can deal face-to-face if they wish. They take delivery of the gold and silver right there on the spot when they pay, so they do not have send money to someone they do not know and have to wait for who-knows-how-long to have their gold sent to them.

During the COVID-19 shutdown, the *Wall Street Journal* coined a new term for gold because so many dealers were incapable of making timely deliveries of gold. They called it "unobtanium." It was not good for the clients of other firms who found they could not get the metals they wanted in a time of crisis without taking unacceptable delivery risks. But it highlighted the capabilities of Republic Monetary Exchange. Right through the period, we were still able to make immediate delivery to all our clients, just as we continue to do every day!

And while we think everyone should protect themselves, their families, and their wealth with precious metals in these times, we know that there are also times people need to sell. Those who need to sell get the same great service and the most competitive prices around, even if they did not buy from us. And they get paid right on the spot, too. That is another part of our "best practices" policy.

As a courtesy to our clients who find it convenient to deal in person at our Phoenix office, we provide on-site security facilitated by the Phoenix Police Department. Our officers provide round-the-clock surveillance, so customers can feel safe during all business transactions at our Phoenix location.

For others, Republic Monetary Exchange offers prompt shipments. Because we have shipped thousands of packages nationwide, our clients can feel safe that their products will be delivered discreetly and securely.

Our signature service includes five-star packaging, fully insured, and expedited shipping.

Those are just some of the reasons people like doing business with Republic Monetary Exchange.

Our website at RMEGold.com will introduce you to a variety of gold and silver coins popular with investors. Visit our blog for timely briefings on the economic environment and latest market conditions. While there, be sure to subscribe to my weekly newsletter that brings all of these latest market updates and articles to your inbox.

I invite anyone to visit us at our long-time location at 4040 East Camelback Road in Phoenix, AZ. For those that are not local to Arizona, call us at 877-354-4040 or chat live with a Precious Metals expert on our website during business hours.

Our mission at RME is to provide our clients with empowering information and help them profit and protect themselves with **real money**... gold and silver.

Whether your goal is to diversify your investments, own physical gold and silver in your IRA, or establish generational wealth, we are here to keep you from being victimized by the Monetary Madmen, the Federal Reserve, and the Deep State.

The Republic Monetary Exchange Offices in Phoenix, AZ

APPENDIX III
ABOUT THE AUTHOR

Jim Clark entered the Precious Metals industry in 1973 when gold was priced at only $45 per ounce. At a young age, he was able to turn a passion for coin collecting into a job. That job quickly became a career. Now over a half-century later, both that passion and his career are stronger than ever.

Jim has traded precious metals in every type of market including many major economic events. He has successfully navigated the markets through ten sitting U.S. Presidents and their vastly different economic policies. As a wholesaler and dealer, more physical metals have traded through his hands than virtually any other individual market-maker in the world.

As an expert in the precious metals market, Jim is often asked to be interviewed and has appeared on national and local news outlets including Fox and NBC. He is also often heard on local radio in his hometown Phoenix market, providing commentary and advice to listeners of market-leading stations KFYI and KTAR. In addition to appearances on television, radio, and podcasts, he has also been invited speak on the panels of national economic conventions like MoneyShow, FreedomFest, and the New Orleans Investment Conference. He is a lifetime member of three of the industry's most respected organizations: The American Numismatic Association (ANA), Professional Coin Grading Services (PCGS), and Numismatic Guaranty Corporation (NGC).

Jim founded Phoenix-based Republic Monetary Exchange in 2008. His goal was to provide the best possible experience for individuals to both buy and sell precious metals. The company quickly grew to a national client base, with physical offices in both Arizona and Colorado. Today, RME is considered a leader in the industry, with excellent client reviews online along with an A+ rating from the Better Business Bureau.

Jim's involvement at RME is deep and pace-setting. While running the overall business as Chief Executive Officer, Jim is actively involved in both buying and selling. Due to his vast knowledge of both American and foreign coins, he acts as the main buyer at RME. His knowledge and foresight of coins, the economy, and the markets have made him a master appraiser with genuine market-setting abilities.

Having been blessed to have such a long and successful lifetime in the industry, Jim decided to document his expert view of gold in America's history by penning this book.

Jim at WOR Studios in New York City.